HEALTHQUEST WEEKEND

May 26-27, 2001

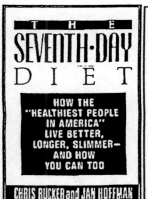

THE SEVENTH·DAY DIET

HOW THE "HEALTHIEST PEOPLE IN AMERICA" LIVE BETTER, LONGER, SLIMMER— AND HOW YOU CAN TOO

CHRIS RUCKER and JAN HOFFMAN

Featuring: Chris Rucker

Co-Author of Random House Publisher's Successful Diet and Fat Management Book, *The Seventh Day Diet*

Sabbath Morning	Sabbath Afternoon
11am	6:00pm
HEALTHQUEST:	HEALTHQUEST:
HOW TO BE ONE OF THE HEALTHIEST PEOPLE IN AMERICA!	HOW TO BE ONE OF THE HEALTHIEST PEOPLE IN AMERICA!
Part 1	Part 2

FAT BUSTERS' COOK-OFF

Sunday, 10:30am - 3:00pm   Donation: $20

A Lowfat, Low Glycemic, Low Calorie, High Fiber, Fun Filled, Fatbusting, Natural "Hands On" Vegetarian Cooking School!

- Hands-On Fat Management Vegetarian Cooking: Learn to Make Fun and Delicious Fatbusting Recipes
- Learn to Follow an easy Fat Management Menu Planner
- Learn to Eliminate Excessive Fat Through Low- Glycemic Indexing

- Learn to Normalize Triglyceride, Cholesterol, Blood Pressure, and Blood Sugar Levels Naturally
- Look Lean: Cut Sugar to Trim Fat with Sugarless Treats
- Tasting Party – Veggie Roast, Entrees, Casseroles, and Desserts

---

May 26-27, 2001
For Cook-Off Reservations
Call: Laura Gilliam @ 219-938-9816

Mizpah S.D.A. Church·
2350 Jefferson St.
Gary, Indiana

THE INSIDE STORY

Jonah

WRESTLING WITH THE GOD OF SECOND CHANCES

JO ANN DAVIDSON

Luaym Bassett
Oct, 2003

REVIEW AND HERALD® PUBLISHING ASSOCIATION
HAGERSTOWN, MD 21740

The author assumes full responsibility for the accuracy of all facts and quotations as cited in this book.

Unless otherwise noted, Bible texts in this book are from the New King James Version. Copyright © 1979, 1980, 1982 by Thomas Nelson, Inc. Used by permission. All rights reserved.

Texts credited to KJV are from the King James Version.

Scripture quotations marked NASB are from the *New American Standard Bible,* copyright © 1960, 1962, 1963, 1968, 1971, 1972, 1973, 1975, 1977, 1994 by The Lockman Foundation. Used by permission.

Scripture quotations marked NLT are taken from the *Holy Bible,* New Living Translation, copyright © 1996. Used by permission of Tyndale House Publishers, Inc., Wheaton, Illinois 60189. All rights reserved.

Bible texts credited to NRSV are from the New Revised Standard Version of the Bible, copyright © 1989 by the Division of Christian Education of the National Council of the Churches of Christ in the U.S.A. Used by permission.

This book was
Edited by Gerald Wheeler
Copyedited by James Cavil
Cover designed by Genesis Design
Cover illustration by Darrel Tank
Interior designed by Freshcut Design
Typeset: Garamond Book 11/14

PRINTED IN U.S.A.

07 06 05 04 03   5 4 3 2 1

R&H Cataloging Service
Davidson, Jo Ann
    Jonah, the inside story.

    1. Bible. O.T. Jonah—Commentaries.   2. Narration in the Bible.
3. Bible. O.T. Jonah—Narrative theology.   I. Title.

                    224.92

ISBN 0-8280-1769-7

To order additional copies of *Jonah: The Inside Story,* by Jo Ann Davidson, call 1-800-765-6955.

Visit us at www.reviewandherald.com for information on other Review and Herald ® products.

DEDICATED TO RICHARD,
MY HUSBAND, MY LOVE, MY BEST FRIEND.
"BLESSED IS THE MAN WHO FEARS THE LORD,
WHO DELIGHTS GREATLY IN HIS COMMANDMENTS. . . .
HE IS GRACIOUS,
AND FULL OF COMPASSION, AND RIGHTEOUS. . . .
HIS HEART IS STEADFAST, TRUSTING IN THE LORD."

—PSALM 112:1-7

CONTENTS

INTRODUCTION

My teenage son Jonathan has been patiently fine-tuning my knowledge of American sports, including playing techniques and game strategies. It has taken some doing, because I have never been particularly interested before. Recently, however, he paid me the supreme compliment that now I know more about sports than the moms of most of his friends! For instance, when it comes to baseball, I now realize that though the game can be played either with a softball or a hardball, both types of ball are *hard* on the head! Jon has also informed me about the differences in batting with a metal or a wooden bat.

And then, of course, there are the distinctions between the major and the minor leagues. Since Jon's birthday is in September, he sometimes wants to celebrate the occasion at a baseball game. But he has never requested to see a game played by a minor league team, such as the South Bend Silver Hawks, even though they play nearby, just across the state line in Indiana. No, he always wants tickets for a Chicago White Sox game. They are in the major leagues! Of course, some great baseball gets played in the minor leagues. But the major leagues is where the most important baseball is played.

The same meaning for the words "major" and "minor" occurs in the field of education. A college student majors in a certain subject or subjects and minors in others. A person's major involves the most work and the most hours in class. The minor is less demanding. And thus the words "major" and "minor" generally mean the difference between the more important and the less important.

However, one must be careful not to employ that customary understanding when studying the Bible. For instance, in the Old Testament we find the "major prophets" and the "minor prophets." One might have the understandable tendency to conclude that the 12 minor prophets just aren't quite as significant as the big major prophets such as Isaiah, Jeremiah, Ezekiel, and Daniel. It is at this point that our understanding of "major" and "minor" must take on a different nuance.

We might consider an analogy in music. Anyone who has had some music lessons recalls that there are both major scales and minor scales. But the designation has nothing to do with the value or importance of the scales. The two types are just structured differently, and the two terms provide a convenient way of classifying them. Likewise in Scripture, the minor prophets are no less important than the major prophets. The former books are just generally shorter. Their length in no way affects their significance, however, for their content is consistently vital and vivid.

We can substantiate this point in the book of Jonah itself, which we will explore in the following pages of this book. Before long we will discover that this little book consisting of only four chapters is definitely not in the minor leagues! The book of Jonah includes much more than just the "great fish," mentioned in only three verses. Jonah contains a major message of paramount importance. And its themes remain very contemporary. Within its 48 verses we will learn about human nature, and thus about ourselves. But most of all, we will expand and deepen our understanding of God.

First of all, however, we must sensitize our reading skills, and increase our appreciation for the Hebrew way of writing narratives or stories. Since narrative writing appears throughout the Bible, including the book of Jonah, such literary awareness is vital for truly grappling with the profound nature of Scripture and especially its theology.

In this study we will work our way through the four chapters of the book of Jonah, frequently verse by verse. We will alert ourselves to key words along with the literary devices and techniques that reveal and underscore the book's theology. And often we will reflect on the implications of that theology. Hopefully, it will become apparent how carefully crafted and constructed the chapters—and even the verses—are. An adventure awaits us!

One

THE HISTORICITY OF JONAH

*P*ause a minute and recall what an astonishingly varied collection of different types of literary materials the Bible contains. One thinks immediately of its stories or narratives and poetry. But that is not all. We find also prophecy and apocalyptic writing, letters both to individual people and also to whole church congregations, liturgical hymns, and even architectural blueprints. Add to that the laws and legal materials. One can even tune into conversations, some short and others lengthy.

These many literary types have attracted much attention and commentary throughout the centuries, starting way back in the time of the Old Testament itself. Later biblical authors refer to and expound on what Moses had composed earlier. The writers of the New Testament frequently provide rich commentary on the Old Testament. Jesus Himself quotes the Old Testament book of Genesis when He discusses marriage and divorce (Matt. 19). Paul often cites poetry from the book of Psalms when he discusses Jesus and His Messiahship. In fact, the minds of all the New Testament writers are steeped in the Old Testament. Peter even refers to Balaam's talking donkey to illustrate his discussion of false teachings then disturbing the church:

"They have forsaken the right way and gone astray, following the way of Balaam the son of Beor, who loved the wages of unrighteousness; but he was rebuked for his iniquity: a dumb donkey speaking with a man's voice restrained the madness of the prophet. These are wells without water, clouds carried by a tempest, for whom is reserved the blackness of darkness forever" (2 Peter 2:15-17).

9

Biblical poetry of both Testaments has long been widely acclaimed, even by those who do not accept Scripture as sacred revelation from God. Many state university literature courses study the profound nature of Hebrew poetry in the Old Testament. It may come as a surprise to some students of Scripture that poetry appears in almost every part of the Bible. Nearly every book in the Old Testament contains some. In fact, up to 40 percent of the Old Testament consists of poetry, including much of the prophetic materials. Even though writers don't often do it, many Bible authors found no difficulty in weaving poetry within the narratives or stories they composed.

Prophetic writings are also a prominent feature in Scripture. In fact, such materials comprise a large proportion of the Old Testament. Modern language translations group the books of Isaiah, Jeremiah, Lamentations, Ezekiel, and Daniel together in what scholars often call the major prophets. The book of Jonah is the fifth of 12 in the collection commonly called the minor prophets, or the Book of the Twelve in the Hebrew Bible. In addition, we find also the "non-writing prophets" such as Elijah, Elisha, and Nathan, among others, in the historical books of the Old Testament.

The many prophetic books, whether major or minor, exhibit a number of similar features. For example, the book of Jonah, like most of the other prophetic books, includes an account of the prophet's life as well as his message. The prophetic books generally consist of the sacred oracles proclaimed by the prophet, with a lesser percentage of biographical material. For example, the book of Isaiah has extensive chapters of prophecy compared with a much lesser amount of narrative details of Isaiah's life. The book of Jonah reverses this proportion. The prophet's prophetic message consists of only a few words: "Yet forty days, and Nineveh shall be overthrown!" (Jonah 3:4). Instead, we find an extended focus on the prophet's life.

Most of the books of the minor prophets also contain biographical material. For example, we read about the time period in which Hosea lived and also his unusual marriage (Hosea 1:1-3). We learn that Amos had another occupation besides that of prophet. He also includes historical markers that indicate the time when he lived, such as naming the ruling monarchs plus mentioning a powerful earthquake (Amos 1:1). Historical details are always present in the books of the prophets, but the amount of such information is often generally brief when compared to the length of the oracles they proclaim.

But the book of Jonah is noticeably different. In it the reader discovers a detailed account of an event in Jonah's personal life. And with its inclusion of supernatural occurrences, the book of Jonah corresponds more closely to the chronicles of the prophets Elijah and Elisha recorded in 1 and 2 Kings.

It should not surprise us that the book links supernatural occurrences with Jonah's life. Such a thing is not unusual for a prophetic ministry. The lives of Elijah and Elisha are similar examples. Some of the miracles that God performed through Elisha include the healing of a spring (2 Kings 2:19-22); the miracle of the widow's oil (2 Kings 4:1-7); the raising of a young boy from the dead (verses 8-37); the stew of poisonous food cured (verses 38-41); the miraculous feeding of many with only a small amount of food (verses 42-44); the healing of leprosy (2 Kings 5:1-19); and the iron ax head floating on water (2 Kings 6:1-7). Miraculous experiences also occur in the prophet Jonah's life. Thus the inclusion of miracles in the book of Jonah is no reason to dismiss it as merely a mythical tale.

Unfortunately, though, modern critics of Scripture dismiss the historicity of the book of Jonah because of its supernatural happenings, such as the "great fish" swallowing Jonah and his remaining alive for three days inside the fish. It is interesting to note, however, that the book refers to such miraculous events only briefly and in a low-key manner. Only three verses mention the "great fish." The same applies to the two winds, the worm, and the plant, all spoken of as under God's control. The writer of the book of Jonah mentions these details unobtrusively in a matter-of-fact manner, as if the reader should not be startled at all to find God's power displayed in such a way. In fact, biblical narratives regularly contain both natural and supernatural elements without any apology or attempt to explain. The writers assume that the sovereign power of the God of heaven makes such events possible. Yet it is these very miraculous features in the text that receive the most extended critique and denial by some modern minds.

The tendency to view Jonah as fictional is a relatively recent development, however. The vast majority of early Jewish and Christian writers believed that the events recorded in the book actually occurred. Among Jewish writers, first-century Josephus, a contemporary of Jesus, clearly viewed the book of Jonah as historical and incorporated the story into his history of the Jewish people: "But, since I have promised to give an exact account of our history, I have thought it necessary to recount what I have found written in the Hebrew books concerning this prophet [Jonah]."[1]

Early Christian writers also viewed Jonah as factual history. They assumed that the book's content reported actual events and was not merely an allegory.[2] The fact that centuries of biblical scholars have believed that the book of Jonah was actual history is impressive. It is only in the modern era that one finds suggestions that the book of Jonah is an ancient myth, a parable, or an allegory—anything but a document of true history.

However, several indicators within the text of the book of Jonah underscore its historical nature. Noticing such details makes one a more careful student of the Bible. In fact, scholars now refer to giving careful attention to textual details as a "close reading of the text." Bible-believing Christians, who have long accepted Scripture as authored by God Himself, should naturally incline toward such a "close reading of the text." They believe that the content of the Bible, though composed of a wide variety of literary materials from many different writers, has been superintended by God Himself and thus portrays a unified worldview. Each book contributes another piece in the extensive biblical mosaic picturing God and His involvement in human history.

An important technique of a "close reading of the text" involves a careful comparison of words and phrases (especially in the original language) within the different biblical books. For example, the book of Jonah begins with the idiomatic expression "now . . . came" *(vayehi)*. This exact phrase also opens many other books of the Old Testament, such as Joshua, Judges, Ruth, 2 Samuel, Esther, and Ezekiel.

Different translations into English of this Hebrew expression may blur this fact, but the identical phrase appears at the outset of each of these and several other historical books in Scripture. Thus, if one accepts Joshua, Ruth, Samuel, Esther, and Ezekiel as actual people who lived in the past, to be consistent Jonah must be too.

English translators often render *vayehi* as "and it came to pass." To some this may suggest fairy-tale content. However, we should never consider "and it came to pass" as the equivalent of "once upon a time" when reading Scripture. This Hebrew term never reflects that kind of meaning. Rather, it indicates that what follows is closely linked to what has already happened. The term can also occur within a book in Scripture to mark a change of events, such as in Ezekiel 3:16, in which it divides Ezekiel's recounting of a vision from a later time period.

Continuing our "close reading" of the book of Jonah, we find that the first verse also reveals that Jonah receives the identical prophetic call that many other biblical prophets did: "Now the word of the Lord came to Jonah" (Jonah 1:1). In the Old Testament it is such a common announcement of the prophetic office that this "introductory formula" should just jump out at us from the text! The very same expression reports the divine summoning of such prophets as Jeremiah, Ezekiel, Hosea, Joel, Micah, Haggai, Zephaniah, and Zechariah, as well as Jonah.

"Then *the word of the Lord* came to me, saying" (Jer. 1:4).

"Moreover *the word of the Lord* came to me, saying" (Jer. 2:1).

"On the fifth day of the month, which was in the fifth year of King Jehoiachin's captivity, *the word of the Lord* came expressly to Ezekiel" (Eze. 1:3).

"*The word of the Lord* that came to Hosea the son of Beeri, in the days of Uzziah" (Hosea 1:1).

"*The word of the Lord* that came to Joel" (Joel 1:1).

"*The word of the Lord* that came to Micah of Moresheth in the days of Jotham, Ahaz, and Hezekiah, kings of Judah" (Micah 1:1).

"*The word of the Lord* which came to Zephaniah . . . in the days of Josiah the son of Amon, king of Judah" (Zeph. 1:1).

"In the second year of King Darius, in the sixth month, on the first day of the month, *the word of the Lord* came by Haggai the prophet" (Haggai 1:1).

"In the eighth month of the second year of Darius, *the word of the Lord* came to Zechariah the son of Berechiah, the son of Iddo the prophet, saying" (Zech. 1:1).

And, of course, Jonah.

Being alert to this Hebrew phrase or formula enables us to become sensitive to the biblical expression of God's calling a prophet in the Old Testament. As we have seen, many of the prophetic books open with "the word of the Lord that came to . . ." In fact, to receive the word of the Lord was the authenticating mark of a true prophet. "Then the Lord appeared again in Shiloh. For the Lord revealed Himself to Samuel in Shiloh *by the word of the Lord*" (1 Sam. 3:21). And Scripture links this prophetic indicator with Jonah more than once:

"He [Jeroboam II] restored the territory of Israel from the entrance of Hamath to the Sea of the Arabah, according to *the word of the Lord* God of Israel, which He had spoken through His servant Jonah the son of Amittai, the prophet who was from Gath Hepher" (2 Kings 14:25).

The fact that we find such verbal linkage repeated in different prophetic books underscores for us that the book of Jonah is a genuine historical record. When other prophetic books open with this introduction we read it as actual information about a real person. To be consistent, we must understand the book of Jonah in the same manner. The use of this one phrase alone assures us that we are not dealing with fairy tales, legends, or myths.

This introductory formula or phrase "the word of the *Lord* came to . . ." also authenticates that the prophetic message that follows does not originate with the prophet, but derives from God Himself. For the text states that it is "the word of the Lord" that comes to each prophet, including Jonah. This is a holy introduction. It should also remind us each time we encounter it in Scripture that we are studying not only people and history, but sacred messages. And we should be filled with awe that the God of heaven would condescend to communicate His holy will with sinful human beings.

The prophetic commissions of Jonah and other Hebrew prophets have additional similarities. Notice how God summons the prophet Elijah and sends him to another city: "The *word of the Lord* came to him [Elijah], saying, '*Arise, go* to Zarephath'" (1 Kings 17:8, 9). On still another occasion *"the word of the Lord came* to Elijah the Tishbite, saying, *'Arise, go* down to meet Ahab king of Israel'" (1 Kings 21:17, 18). The prophet Jeremiah receives a corresponding injunction when God commands him: *"Arise, go* to the Euphrates . . ." "Then I went to the Euphrates . . ." the prophet recalls (Jer. 13:4-7). God summons the prophet Jonah in the same way: *"The word of the Lord came* to Jonah the son of Amittai, saying, *'Arise, go* to Nineveh'" (Jonah 1:1, 2).

The divine mandate is verbally identical for Elijah, Jeremiah, and Jonah, again underscoring the historical nature of the book of Jonah. If we accept the historicity of Elijah and Jeremiah, Scripture links Jonah's prophetic ministry to theirs in this obviously parallel manner.

We can further establish the historicity of the book of Jonah by noticing how the Old Testament flanks it with two unquestioned prophetic books, Obadiah and Micah. The fact that Jonah is in the "Book of the Twelve," as the Hebrew Bible names the minor prophets, helps us to understand why no one questioned its content as historical for so many centuries. Even the position of the book of Jonah within the grouping of the 12 minor prophets reveals a broadly historical sequence.

Moreover, Jonah delivers a message that is obviously prophetic in nature, dealing with the same issues of destruction and restoration fundamental to all biblical prophets. For example, Old Testament prophets insist that the city of Jerusalem, as with the city of Nineveh, is destined for destruction if no genuine repentance takes place. And we will find that Yahweh will draw on His infinite stores of mercy to delay or defer judgment for both cities. The book of Jonah contains historical prophecy as genuine as any other in the Old Testament.

Another indicator that serves to establish the factual nature of the book of Jonah appears in its very literary style. Again this involves noticing what might seem to be insignificant details as we continue our close reading of the text. The book refers to Jonah in the third person, a trait typical of prophetic writing in the Old Testament. The prophets often speak of themselves in the third person.

For example, we find the prophet Amos answering and pleading with God. Note how Amos relates in first person the words God spoke to him in vision:

"Thus the Lord God showed me"; "And so it was . . . that I said"; "Thus He showed me"; "And the Lord said to me"; "And I said"; "Thus the Lord God showed me"; "And He said, 'Amos, what do you see?' So I said" (Amos 7:1–8:2). Yet, as you read further in the book of Amos, he also refers to himself in the third person.

Isaiah also speaks of himself in the third person when reporting how God sent him to meet Ahaz: "And it was told to the house of David, saying, 'Syria's forces are deployed in Ephraim.' So his heart and the heart of his people were moved as the trees of the woods are moved with the wind" (Isa. 7:2).

The prophet Ezekiel also moves back and forth between first and third person:

"Now it came to pass in the thirtieth year, in the fourth month, on the fifth day of the month, as I was among the captives by the River Chebar, that the heavens were opened and I saw visions of God. On the fifth day of the month, which was in the fifth year of King Jehoiachin's captivity, *the word of the Lord* came expressly to Ezekiel the priest, the son of Buzi, in the land of the Chaldeans by the River Chebar; and the hand of the Lord was upon him there. Then I looked" (Eze. 1:1-4).

We find the same phenomenon in the book of Jeremiah. And, as we might expect, the book of Jonah has the entire narrative written in third person.

Another important issue in the book of Jonah that needs our attention is the prominent inclusion of a Gentile nation. Other prophetic books also feature divine oracles to nations outside Israel. Isaiah's oracles include Assyria, Babylon, Philistia, Moab, Syria, Ethiopia, and Egypt (Isa. 9; 10;13-24). Jeremiah prophesies about Egypt, Philistia, Moab, Ammon, Edom, Damascus, and Babylon (Jer. 46-51). Ezekiel's prophetic messages address Babylon, Philistia, Ammon, Edom, Tyre, Sidon, and Egypt (Eze. 25-32). God even directs a second prophet to Nineveh:

"The burden against Nineveh. The book of the vision of Nahum the Elkoshite. . . . 'Behold, I am against you,' says the Lord of hosts, 'I will burn your chariots in smoke. . . . Woe to the bloody city! It is all full of lies and robbery" (Nahum 1:1–3:1).

God discloses His concern for all nationalities long before the New Testament. Even the original covenant given to Abraham back in Genesis included the nations of the world: "I will make you a great nation; I will bless you and make your name great; and you shall be a blessing. . . . And *in you all the families of the earth shall be blessed"* (Gen. 12:2, 3). Thus we should not be astonished when God directs Jonah to Nineveh.

Another key undergirds the historical nature of Jonah. The book includes many references to God. Indeed, we will find Him rather than Jonah as the central focus of the four-chapter narrative or story. This is a critical issue. Considering the reverence for God and even His name that Jewish tradition holds, it seems highly improbable that the Hebrew Bible would include a fictional account, myth, or legend that featured God so prominently.

Other important historical markers include the writer's linking the story to then-prominent places such as the city of Tarshish and the city of Nineveh, a common feature of Old Testament narratives. All through the Hebrew Bible we find geographical details punctuating the narratives. For example, we find the biblical writers naming rocks, fields, and even trees and tagging them to events. One of many examples is the cave that Abraham bought: "Abraham weighed out the silver for Ephron which he had named in the hearing of the sons of Heth, four hundred shekels of silver, currency of the merchants. So the field of Ephron which was in Machpelah, which was before Mamre, the field and the cave which was in it, and all the trees that were in the field, which were within all the surrounding borders, were deeded to Abraham as a possession in the presence of the sons of Heth, before all who went in at the gate of his city. And after this, Abraham buried Sarah his wife *in the cave of the field of Machpelah, before Mamre (that is, Hebron) in the land of Canaan"* (Gen. 23:16-19).

Later the book of Judges locates Deborah's "judgment seat" geographically: "Now Deborah, a prophetess, the wife of Lapidoth, was judging Israel at that time. And she would sit under the *palm tree of Deborah between Ramah and Bethel in the mountains of Ephraim.* And the children of Israel came up to her for judgment" (Judges 4:4, 5). The city of Nineveh features prominently in the book of Jonah, paralleling this use of geography to reinforce historicity.

Moreover, we find Jonah's life attested elsewhere in the Old Testament, situating him both historically and geographically: "In the fifteenth year of Amaziah the son of Joash, king of Judah, Jeroboam the son of Joash, king of Israel, became king in Samaria, and reigned forty-one years. . . . He restored the territory of Israel from the entrance of Hamath to the Sea of the Arabah, according to the word of the Lord God of Israel, which He had spoken through His servant Jonah the son of Amittai, *the prophet who was from Gath Hepher*" (2 Kings 14:23-25).

Some have even suggested that because the writer does not name the king, the book of Jonah is a fictional story. However, in the biblical narratives, an unnamed royal figure does not connote fictionality. Scripture does not name the Egyptian pharaoh of the Exodus, either. "Pharaoh" is a title, not the name of the monarch. The same thing happens again in the book of Jonah.

Throughout the modern era, scholars have also variously considered the book of Jonah as allegory or a parable because of the skillful use of irony throughout. However, life itself is filled with irony! Human experiences regularly involve incongruities, and things often do not turn out even with the best-laid plans. The recognition of irony in the book of Jonah is not reason enough to classify it as a fairy tale.

The writer of the book of Jonah obviously intended that we understand it as genuine history. As we have just seen, it contains numerous historical links. Furthermore, a narrative or story in Scripture is a historical record. The Bible writers again and again include links of actual places and times to anchor their narrative materials. By this they underscore that what they write is factual.

In the New Testament Jesus Himself speaks of the prophet Jonah and links His own mission to the prophet's experience. In fact, Jonah is the only prophet that Christ does this with. And He also directly associates Jonah with the historical city of Nineveh:

"Then some of the scribes and Pharisees answered, saying, 'Teacher, we want to see a sign from You.' But He answered and said to them, 'An evil and adulterous generation seeks after a sign, and no sign will be given to it except the sign of the prophet Jonah. For as Jonah was three days and three nights in the belly of the great fish, so will the Son of Man be three days and three nights in the heart of the earth. The men of Nineveh will rise up in the judgment with this generation and condemn it, because they repented at the preaching of Jonah; and indeed a greater than Jonah is here" (Matt. 12:38-41; see also Luke 11:29-32).

Taking the Bible as a whole, including the vast number of stories or narratives, some regard the Jewish people as having almost an obsession with history. The different Old Testament Bible writers were always referring to their past history and tying it to local places and events. Their historical memory was vital to them. We have no other known historical records from any other ancient country that are so distinctly grounded in such extensive historical details and records. It is almost as if the Bible writers are urging their readers to check out the veracity of what they are writing about. All through the Old Testament the biblical writers even explain the origin of familiar customs:

"Again the Lord spoke to Moses, saying, 'Speak to the children of Israel: Tell them to make tassels on the corners of their garments throughout their generations, and to put a blue thread in the tassels of the corners. And you shall have the tassel, that you may look upon it and remember all the commandments of the Lord and do them'" (Num. 15:38, 39).

Scripture also traces ancient names and current sayings back to their origins: "And he called the name of that place Bethel; but the name of that city had been Luz previously" (Gen. 28:19).

We could cite many other examples, such as:

"It came to pass the same day that Isaac's servants came and told him about the well which they had dug, and said to him, 'We have found water.' So he called it Shebah. Therefore the name of the city is Beersheba to this day" (Gen. 26:32, 33).

The Old Testament links divine commands to specific niches in history:

"Then the Lord said to Joshua, 'This day I have rolled away the reproach of Egypt from you.' Therefore the name of the place is called Gilgal to this day" (Joshua 5:9).

Biblical writers regularly provide personal names, family ties, and geographical data, as if to suggest that the readers should check out the details for themselves. The narratives of Moses in the book of Genesis offer representative examples. Consider the following: "Now Moses was tending the flock of Jethro his father-in-law, the priest of Midian. And he led the flock to the back of the desert, and came to Horeb, the mountain of God" (Ex. 3:1).

All of this attention to detail anchors the biblical narratives or stories in public and verifiable features of human history. Such details combine to underscore the veracity of the incidents the biblical writers record. It is as if they are insisting that we can trust their accounting of history.

In fact, many scholars now recognize the ancient Jewish writers as the first to write historical narratives or stories with the account moving steadily forward in time, having a beginning and an end. While some scholars call the Greek Herodotus the "father of history," the Old Testament records appeared much earlier.

It is significant that recent studies in theology have again returned to the biblical narrative, recognizing it not only as exquisitely crafted material, but also as contributing significantly to historical and theological studies in Scripture. It is to the specialized qualities of biblical narratives that we now turn.

---

[1] Josephus *Jewish Antiquities* 9. 10. 2.
[2] R. H. Bowers, *The Legend of Jonah* (The Hague: Martinus Hijhoff, 1971), pp. 20-32.

Two

THE LITERARY NATURE OF BIBLICAL NARRATIVES

In the past few decades, as the understanding of the ancient Hebrew language has become more sophisticated, scholars have increasingly paid attention to the literary qualities of the biblical narratives or stories. Earlier in the past century many had dismissed the frequent verbal repetitions within the biblical narratives as indicating a primitive, unsophisticated type of writing. They especially viewed the Old Testament narratives or stories as merely a collection of many disparate myths and legends, written and compiled much later than the time period implied in the text. Then later different anonymous "editors" supposedly assembled the collections together. They also likely added their own comments in the process. All this, the scholars conjectured, produced the obvious repetitions in the text. Each Old Testament book supposedly had multiple authors. And the history recorded in the narratives was not considered reliable, if it even happened at all.

Even a large part of the Christian world has accepted such reasoning. Seventh-day Adventists, however, have always believed that the historical materials in Scripture, including the narratives, though not exhaustive history, are nevertheless recording true history.

Increasing sensitivity to the Hebrew language in the past few decades of the twentieth century has especially heightened our appreciation for the biblical narratives. In fact, scholars are increasingly recognizing Hebrew narratives as highly sophisticated writing that reflects careful and thoughtful construction. And it is attention to the seemingly "minor" details contained within the narratives that earlier scholars scoffed at that has brought about this belated recognition.

For example, a close reading of biblical narratives will clearly make apparent the characteristic verbal repetitions. The style of writing is so different from what is customary today in writing history that it is understandable why earlier critics relegated biblical narratives to nonhistorical legends.

However, it is these very repetitions that scholars now increasingly recognize and appreciate as the distinctly Hebrew manner of writing historical narratives or stories. Such repetitions serve as a deliberate manner of emphasis and theological expression. Scholars now rightly acknowledge biblical narratives as intricately written literary masterpieces despite their seemingly simple expression. Biblical authors obviously intended their narratives primarily for thoughtful adult readers and not merely as stories for children.

Not only that, scholars now see biblical narratives as carefully linked together in calculated sequences and not merely a haphazard collection of tales. Not only are the writer's choice of words and repetitions (previously often ridiculed) now increasingly appreciated, but even the actual juxtaposition of the narratives to each other is perceived as carefully arranged. For example, critics long regarded the narrative of Tamar and Judah as an awkward insertion in the Joseph narratives in Genesis. But its precise location yields a theological significance that earlier scholars missed.

There also seem to be theological reasons that the New Testament narrative of the woman at Samaria's well (John 4) follows immediately after that of Nicodemus seeking the Messiah late one night (John 3). The apostle John, though writing in Greek, was a Hebrew, and he continues within the Old Testament narrative tradition as he writes. Thus he subtly compares the hesitant faith in Christ of a prominent Jewish religious leader with that of an eager non-Israelite divorcée! In fact, throughout the entire Gospel, John pairs narratives in just this manner to contrast the faith or unbelief of those involved. John makes implicit comparisons through such narrative linkages rather than by explicit statements, as a contemporary writer might.

It is only fair to the biblical writers that we read their narrative materials with a sensitivity to their style of writing. Then we can probe the Bible more intelligently for its theological depth. Let us spend a little time reviewing a few of what we now understand as the typical literary features of biblical narratives.

1. *Repetition of words and phrases.* We have already briefly mentioned verbal repetitions. Since they form so conspicuous a part of biblical narratives they deserve more attention. Noticing a few will sensitize our reading skills. For example, Allan Coppedge remarks on the textual repetitions recording the creation of Adam and Eve:

"The climax of the story of creation in Genesis 1 deals with the making of man and woman. Having created the universe and all other forms of life, God surveys his work and declares that it is good (Gen. 1:25). Then he says, 'Let us make man in our image, after our likeness'; . . . So God created man in his own image, in the image of God he created him; male and female he created them" (verses 26, 27). Apparently the writer of the story thought it was particularly significant that God created individuals in his own image. He emphasizes this fact by repeating the phrase. The uniqueness of this part of creation is further highlighted by the fact that this is the only part of creation that is described as being made like God."[1]

Notice in the narrative of Genesis 4 the repetition of the word "brother." Read the story with just this one detail in mind and observe how many times it reminds the reader that Cain and Abel are brothers. Contemporary literary authors might record such an account differently, pointing out explicitly the horrifying fact that the first murder in Scripture involved fratricide when Cain killed his own brother. But the ancient Hebrew way of writing draws attention to this more indirectly by repeating again and again that the two men involved were brothers, thus choosing to underscore the heinous nature of the crime in this haunting manner.

Another example of the characteristic verbal repetitions in biblical narratives or stories appears in the story of Rahab (Joshua 6). Notice how often it mentions her as a prostitute. The passage repeatedly describes her as "Rahab the harlot" (or "prostitute") when it might seem to the modern mind that one reference to her "profession" would be enough (see also Hebrews 11:31 in this respect). But we must allow ancient writers to express themselves as they do and not expect that they reflect our Western modes, even if it is very different than what we are used to. In the case of Rahab, the writer of the book of Joshua just might have been seeking to emphasize the nature of God's grace that excludes no one, no matter how shady their past.

We could review thousands of such examples throughout all the biblical narratives. In fact, it is one of the most prominent features of biblical narrative writing. Not surprisingly, we will encounter this technique used again and again in the book of Jonah.

2. Use of dialogue. Another important literary feature of biblical narratives are the dialogues. In a biblical story the writers typically present a sequence of events occurring in time. However, at certain points they sometimes punctuate this progression with dialogue. When this happens the narrative time "slows down" with the inserted conversation.

Narrative dialogue in Scripture is striking for its consistency of style. You will never find several people in a group conversing. Most often only two talk, with three the limit. We will find this true in the book of Jonah as well.

In biblical narrative dialogues, not only what is said is important, but who is speaking, whether named or not. For example, in Jonah 4 we find the prophet and God conversing with each other. In Genesis 3 we find Adam, Eve, and God talking together. God speaks with Adam first, and then with Eve. Queen Esther, King Ahasuerus, and Haman speak alternately to each other in Esther 7. And we listen to Samuel and King Saul in conversation in 1 Samuel 15. As skills in close readings of the text have increased, scholars now recognize that the conversations represent pivotal points in the story.

Sometimes the author will repeat an entire conversation at a later juncture in the narrative, underscoring its importance, such as when Nathan instructs Bathsheba what to tell King David. The narrator records her as repeating Nathan's as she speaks to David, rather than just commenting that she told David what Nathan had said to her (1 Kings 1). Other times the writer will mention that a conversation has occurred without repeating its exact words, such as in the narrative of David, Abigail, and Nabal:

"When David heard in the wilderness that Nabal was shearing his sheep, David sent ten young men; and David said to the young men,

'Go up to Carmel, go to Nabal, and greet him in my name. And thus you shall say to him who lives in prosperity: 'Peace be to you, peace to your house, and peace to all that you have! Now I have heard that you have shearers. Your shepherds were with us, and we did not hurt them, nor was there anything missing from them all the while they were in Carmel. Ask your young men, and they will tell you. Therefore let my young men find favor in your eyes, for we come on a feast day. Please give whatever comes to your hand to your servants and to your son David.' So when David's young men came, *they spoke to Nabal according to all these words in the name of David,* and waited" (1 Sam. 25:4-9).

The same thing happens when God instructs Nathan how to respond to David's desire to build God a house. After God's extensive communication to Nathan (2 Sam. 7:4-16), the narrator does not record all that Nathan said to David, but merely states: "According to all these words and according to all this vision, so Nathan spoke to David" (verse 17).

Another example finds God instructing the prophet Ahijah "thus and thus," which Ahijah later expresses in its entirety:

"Now the Lord had said to Ahijah, 'Here is the wife of Jeroboam, coming to ask you something about her son, for he is sick. *Thus and thus* you shall say to her; for it will be, when she comes in, that she will pretend to be another woman.' And so it was, when Ahijah heard the sound of her footsteps as she came through the door, he said, 'Come in, wife of Jeroboam. Why do you pretend to be another person? For I have been sent to you with bad news. Go, tell Jeroboam, "Thus says the Lord God of Israel" ' " (1 Kings 14:5-7).

Perceptive readers note these different methods of recording dialogue and conversation and use them to enhance their understanding of the narrative.

3. *Literary structures.* Biblical narratives often exhibit literary structures such as "envelope writing," "mirror writing," or "chiasms." These features naturally highlight key points or theological issues that the writer wants to emphasize in the narrative. The distinctive pattern of "mirror writing," sometimes referred to as a "chiasm," is the use of certain key words, phrases, or themes that lead up to the main

point that will be found in the structural center of that particular passage. Following this, the author repeats the same key words, phrases, or themes, but now in reverse order, "framing" or "enveloping" the important central point the writer wishes to highlight.

"Mirror writing," or chiasms, can occur in single verses, a several-verse passage, or even whole chapters and books. In fact, the entire Pentateuch, the first five books of the Bible, containing a vast collection of narratives, has been shown to be a "macrochiasm," or a large-scale chiasm. It has been seen that the main themes of the book of Genesis appear again in the book of Deuteronomy. The same thing happens with the principal themes of the book of Exodus, which the book of Numbers recapitulates. The book of Leviticus carries the focal point of the whole Pentateuch, with its own center found in chapter 16 with the Day of Atonement, as shown below:

A Genesis
> **B** Exodus
>> **C** *Leviticus* 1-7, Sanctuary Laws
>>> **D** *Leviticus* 8-10, Priestly Laws
>>>> **E** *Leviticus* 11-15, Personal Laws
>>>>> **F** *Leviticus* 16, DAY OF ATONEMENT
>>>> **E'** *Leviticus* 17-20, Personal Laws
>>> **D'** *Leviticus* 21, 22, Priestly Laws
>> **C'** *Leviticus* 23-27, Sanctuary Laws
> **B'** Numbers

A' Deuteronomy[2]

Many Old Testament narratives employ this type of literary structure. Let us notice just a few to become sensitive to them:

1. Genesis 2:4–3:24:

A Narrative: <u>God, man from *adamah* to garden</u> (2:4b-17)
> **B** Narrative: <u>God, man, woman, animals relationships among creatures</u> (2:18-25)
>> **C** Dialogue: serpent, woman *eating from the tree*
>>> three statements (3:1-5)
>>> **D** Narrative: woman, man *eating from the tree* (3:6-8)
>> **C'** Dialogue: God, man, woman
>>> *eating from the tree*

three questions/answers (3:9-13)

B' Monologue: <u>God, man, woman, serpent relationships among creatures</u> (3:14-19)

A' Narrative: <u>God, man from garden to *adamah*</u> (3:20-24)

The structure is very apparent. The Bible includes at its outset a significant chiasm that places the fall of Adam and Eve at its center.

2. Genesis 6-9:

The Flood narrative reveals chiastic ordering, with the writer highlighting God's grace within the overwhelming Flood event:

1. "My covenant with you" (6:11-22)

  2. Clean animals (7:1-5)

    3. Clean animals (7:6-10)

      4. Enters ark (7:11-16)

        5. The Flood

          6. The Flood rises (7:17-24); seven verbs of "ascent"

            7. <u>The Flood crests</u>

            <u>The ark rests</u>

            <u>God remembers Noah (8:1-5)</u>

          6'. The Flood abates (8:6-12); seven verbs of "descent"

        5'. After the Flood

      4'. Exits the ark (8:13-19)

    3'. Noah's sacrifice (8:20-22)

  2'. Noah's diet (9:1-7)

1'. "My covenant with you" (9:8-17)

3. God's speech in Exodus 6:2-8 offers another example of theological emphasis framed in literary structure:

And God spoke unto Moses, and said unto him:

A *I am the Lord*

  B And I appeared unto *Abraham, Isaac, and Jacob* as God Almighty, but as My name the Lord was I not known to them.

    C And also I have established My covenant with them, to give them *the land* of Canaan, the land of their pilgrimage wherein they were strangers.

      D And also I have heard the *groaning* of the children of Israel, whom the *Egyptians keep in bondage* and I have remembered My covenant.

> **E** Say therefore to the children of Israel: *I am the Lord* and I will release you from *the burdens of Egypt;* and deliver you from their *bondage,* and redeem you with arm outstretched, and with great judgments. And will take you to be My people, and I will be your God and you shall know that *I the Lord am your God.*
> **D'** who release you from the *burdens of Egypt*
> **C'** And I will bring you to *the land,* concerning which I swore with uplifted hand to give
> **B'** to *Abraham, Isaac, and Jacob;* and I will give it to you for a heritage:
> **A'** *I am the Lord.*

Note the corresponding themes on either side of the most important point that comes in the center (E). The whole passage opens and closes with the refrain 'I (am) the Lord.' Second comes a reference to the patriarchs who were the first to experience divine revelation. Accordingly the passage refers to them again in the last phrase. The Promised Land is mentioned again in the third position before the reference to the patriarchs. Fourth comes the bondage and, likewise, fourth from the end, the author repeats the theme. The divine recapitulation of these themes in the "burdens of Egypt" at the center underscores the significance of God's speech. A major factor contributing to the sublime and majestic tone of the whole passage is the fourfold refrain "I am the Lord," each time appearing at a strategic point.[3]

4. Scholars have frequently noted the masterful literary composition of the book of Esther. Sandra Berg suggests the following overall structure:

A. Opening and background (1)
   B. The king's first decree (2; 3)
      C. Clash between Haman and Mordecai (4; 5)
         D. Turning point: "That night the king could not sleep" (6:1)
      C'. Mordecai's triumph over Haman (6; 7)
   B'. The king's second decree (8; 9)
A'. Epilogue (10)[4]

Berg continues by describing how "the second part of the scroll repeats the first not only in content and structure, but also in its episodes, keywords, idioms and stylistic techniques. For example, three banquets are found prior to the central verse of 6:1, just as three feasts follow. We find three references to the royal chronicles at the beginning (2:23), middle (6:1) and end (10:2) of the scroll. In addition several key words occur the same number of times in the first and second halves of the scroll. . . . The book of Esther was constructed according to a precise pattern that manifests the theme of reversal." [5]

Chiasms are prominent throughout both the Old and New Testaments. The canon closes with the book of Revelation, which also includes dramatic chiasms that can assist the reader in unlocking the theological treasures of that book. For example, the vision of the seven churches commences with a chiastic structure:

A "One like the Son of Man. . . . His eyes like a flame of fire; His feet were like fine brass" (1:13-15)

  B "Out of His mouth went a sharp two-edged sword" (1:16)

    C "I am the First and the Last. I am He who lives, and I was dead, and behold, I am alive" (1:17, 18)

      D "The mystery of the seven stars which you saw in My right hand, and the seven golden lampstands" (1:20)

      D' To Ephesus: "These things say He who holds the seven stars in His right hand, who walks among the seven golden lampstands" (2:1)

    C' To Smyrna: "These things says the First and the Last, who was dead, and came to life" (2:8)

  B' To Pergamus: "These things says He who has the sharp two-edged sword" (2:12)

A' To Thyatira: "These things says the Son of God, who has eyes like a flame of fire, and His feet like fine brass" (2:18) [6]

When mirror writing is present, it can furnish a key to the central message of the passage. It illuminates the relationships between seemingly repetitious sections and even the links between the narratives. Chiasms often order otherwise seemingly incoherent materials, underscoring the central meaning of the text under study. Mirror writing provides insight into an ancient way of thinking and writing that the modern mind easily overlooks because it has been conditioned differently. Unlike the Hebrews, we more often think syllogistically and seek to avoid repetitiveness.

For example, English compositions often place the main point at the end. This practice contrasts with biblical materials, where the climax of a section, chapter, or book often comes in the very center of the passage, with the main themes leading up to the climax. These same themes then reappear after the pivotal point, only in reverse order, now informed by the main point the writer sought to make. Mirror writing and chiasms are such a prominent literary feature of biblical writing, including the narratives, that we cannot emphasize too strongly the importance of becoming alert to them!

Thus it should not surprise us that we find a typical example in the opening verses of the book of Jonah: "But Jonah arose to flee to Tarshish from the presence of the Lord. He went down to Joppa, and found a ship going to Tarshish; so he paid the fare, and went down into it, to go with them to Tarshish from the presence of the Lord" (Jonah 1:3).

Let us pause and probe this verse for its literary treasures. It seems so uncomplicated and elementary at first glance. But alert readers will notice the little repetitions in the verse that may seem unnecessary at first reading. For example, is the writer or narrator carelessly "stuttering" when he twice repeats the phrase "from the presence of the Lord"? And why does he indicate *three times* in just that one verse that Jonah is going to Tarshish? Is that repetition really necessary?

The writer is not sloppy or stuttering. Nor are later "editors" adding their comments. Instead the biblical author is alerting us to something important that the reader should ponder. In this case, the triple mention of the city of Tarshish should compel us to notice that Jonah is traveling in a direction diametrically opposite his divine directive!

Nineveh is 500 miles east from Jonah's home. But Tarshish is 2,000 miles west. Thus this one verse points out *three* times the nature of Jonah's rebellion. Perhaps the prophet decided to sail to Tarshish because it was an outpost of Phoenician trade and as far away as he could go. Perhaps it was the distance more than the destination, for Tarshish was far west from Nineveh, a city way to the east from Israel. The stress on the ship's destination is vital to the reader's understanding of Jonah's character.

This striking repetition in just one single verse also alerts us to the possibility of mirror writing, the distinctive style of writing that we have just mentioned. If present here, this literary structure could assist us in understanding the meaning the writer intended to emphasize. Notice how the repeated words in Jonah 1:3 form a chiastic pattern:

> **A** But Jonah arose to flee *to **Tarshish*** from *the presence of the Lord*.
>> **B** He <u>went down</u> to Joppa,
>>> **C** and found a ship
>>>> **D** going to ***Tarshish;***
>>> **C'** so he paid the fare,
>> **B'** and <u>went down</u> into it,
> **A'** to go with them *to **Tarshish** from <u>the presence of the Lord.</u>*

In addition to the triple mention of Tarshish, notice the repetition of the phrase "from the presence of the Lord" found at both the beginning and the end of this one verse. Perhaps the writer wanted to point out the irony of a person—and particularly a prophet—who assumes that escape from God is even possible.

Furthermore, twice in just this one verse the author tells us that Jonah "went down." Thus the writer directs the reader's attention to the downward trend of Jonah's rebellious journey. Three times in close succession the reader learns that Jonah went "down . . . down . . . down" in seeking to avoid his divine task.

In addition to mirror writing, Scripture contains another type of literary structure called "panel writing." Often employed in biblical narrative writing, it also involves repetition of key words and themes. But the repetitions, instead of being reversed, now in appear in the same order in the second appearance. Such "panels" occur in the prophetic oracles as well as the narratives. Notice the structure of certain sections of the book of Ezekiel (1-11 and 40-48):

Yahweh Comes to His Temple panel structure:[7]

1. Dateline: Unique double-dating "The hand of the Lord was upon him" "visions of God" (1:1-13)	1. Dateline: Unique double-dating "The hand of the Lord was upon me" "visions of God" (40:1, 2a)
2. Glory of God comes from the north (to the south) (1:4a)	2. Ezekiel looks (from the north) to the south (40:2b)
3. Description of cultic entities: cherubim and chariot-throne (1:4b-26a)	3. Description of cultic entities: the new temple and its chambers (40:3–42:20)
4. Coming of the glory of the Lord (1:26b-28a)	4. Coming of the glory of the Lord (43:1-9)
5. Ezekiel falls on his face and is lifted up by the Spirit (1:28b–2:2)	5. Ezekiel falls on his face and is lifted up by the Spirit (43:3, 5)
6. Commissioning of Ezekiel (2:3–3:27)	6. Recommissioning of Ezekiel (43:10, 11; cf. 40:4)
7. Indictments for breaking covenant stipulations: abominations of false worship at the Temple (4-8)	7. New covenant stipulations: "the law of the temple" for proper worship (43:12–46:24)
8. Divine glory pauses at the threshold of the Temple, then moves to the east (9:1–11:13; especially 9:3; 10:4, 18, 19)	8. Healing water (symbolizing the divine presence) comes from under the threshold of the Temple and flows to the east (47:1-12)
9. Promised restoration of the land (11:14-21)	9. Borders of the restored land (47:13-48:29)
10. Departure of the glory of God from the city (11:22-25)	10. God does not depart: the city is named "the Lord is there" (48:30-35)

The overall compositional structure of the book of Jonah has directly parallel complements as well. Notice how the author has arranged the two major sections of the book in panel writing:

Part One	*Part Two*
"Arise, go to Nineveh" (1:2)	"Arise, go to Nineveh" (3:2)
Jonah evades his mission by fleeing to the west (1:3)	Jonah fulfills his mission by going to the east (3:3)
God's intervention by means of	God's intervention by means of
(a) a storm (1:4)	(a) a tiny animal (4:7)
(b) a huge animal (2:1)	(b) a wind (4:8)
"But Jonah arose" (1:3)	"So Jonah arose" (3:3)
The sailors pray (1:5)	The people believe (3:5)
The captain's speech (1:6)	The king's decree (3:7)
Shall all perish so that one be punished?	Shall all perish so that one be vindicated?
Three days (1:17)	Three days (3:3)
He prays for his life (2:2)	He prays for his death (4:3)
Divine name 17 times	Divine name 18 times
YHWH Elohim (once, 1:9)	YHWH Elohim (once, 4:6)

These subtle literary pairings are powerfully evocative and extensively distributed all through the biblical narrative materials. They may appear in a single verse, a whole chapter, or sometimes within an entire book, such as that of Jonah and Ezekiel. Becoming sensitive to such characteristic repetitions and literary structures as mirror and panel writing gives the reader of Scripture a better feel for Hebrew writing and thinking. And even though the New Testament was written in Greek, only one writer wasn't a Hebrew! Thus it is not surprising to find such literary patterns all throughout the New Testament, also.

For example, Christ's parable of the two sons (Luke 15:11-32) highlights through its structure the father's compassion:

A One son takes his inheritance; conversation between father and son (verses 11, 12)

  B One son goes out; his conduct (verses 13-16)

    C The well-being of the father's servants recalled; "I perish" (verse 17)

      D I will say, "I have sinned" (verses 18, 19)

        E the father runs to meet his son and is compassionate (verse 20)

> **D'** The son says, "I have sinned" (verse 21)
>> **C'** The father instructs the servants to make well; the lost is found (verses 22-24)
> **B'** One son refuses to go in; his conduct (verses 25-30)

A' One son promised his inheritance; conversation between father and son about it (verses 31, 32)[8]

Even the entire book of Hebrews is carefully structured:

A Jesus is forever (1:8), so great a salvation we cannot neglect (2:3), who is a Son higher than the angels, whose house is more glorious than that of Moses (1:1–3:7)

> **B** The word preached unto the house of Israel did not profit them because they hardened their hearts and had no faith upon their day of temptation (3:7–4:13)

>> **C** Christ's priesthood is higher than that of Aaron or of the Levitical priests (4:14–7:28)

>>> **D** We have a high priest who officiates in the sanctuary built by God (8:1, 2)

>> **C'** Christ's covenant is the eternal testament higher than the atonement administered in the Temple by the Levites (8:3–10:35)

> **B'** The word preached to some did profit them by faith as they became heirs of righteousness and obtained good report by pleasing God (10:36–11:40)

A' Jesus is forever (13:8), a great witness that we cannot neglect (12:1) as we become sons (12:7-9) in Christ's house, which is the heavenly Jerusalem (12:22-28).[9]

As we mentioned earlier, many critics of Scripture have assumed that the extensively distributed verbal repetitions were unnecessary and even indicated incompetence on the part of the writers. Within the past few decades, however, scholars have increasingly appreciated the extent of mirror writing and panel writing in the canon. Instead of regarding them as resulting from amateur skill, they now more correctly perceive such characteristic repetitions and literary structures as expressions of highly sophisticated writing. And they see in them evidence of theological reflection and compositional eloquence through which a biblical writer highlights or underscores a significant issue.

4. *Use of irony.* One other prominent literary tool in biblical narratives that we need to consider is the use of irony. For example, the book of Jonah reveals sophisticated irony as it subtly discloses what kind of person Jonah really is. Instead of direct characterization, as done in much modern writing, the book of Jonah compares the prophet first with the pagan sailors, then with the Gentile Ninevites. Later we will note how the author actually presents these intriguing points of comparison.

The entire book of Jonah is an example of impressive narrative writing. The very structuring of its materials, along with the repetition of certain key words and the use of mirror or panel writing in addition to pointed irony, reveals its theological treasures and calls forth admiration from all those who take time to probe its depths. As we give careful study to its 48 verses, we will see that the writer has enclosed the profound theological message of the book of Jonah in a literary masterpiece.

In the rest of this book we will probe the narrative of the book of Jonah through careful attention to the textual details. We will discover that it includes important theological issues, such as repentance, judgment, divine mercy, salvation, biblical prayer, and even ecology. And when we are through, the ancient book of Jonah will seem surprisingly contemporary. Even more important, we will learn vital lessons for our own walk with God.

---

[1] Allan Coppedge, *Portraits of God: A Biblical Theology of Holiness* (Downers Grove, Ill.: InterVarsity Press, 2001), pp. 66, 67.

[2] Richard M. Davidson, "Assurance in the Judgment," *Adventist Review,* Jan. 7, 1988, pp. 18-20. The structure of Leviticus is adapted from William Shea, "Literary Form and Theological Function in Leviticus," in *The Seventy Weeks, Leviticus and the Nature of Prophecy,* ed. Frank B. Holbrook (Washington, D.C.: Biblical Research Institute, 1986), pp. 139-149.

[3] Nehama Leibowitz, *Studies in Shemot: The Book of Exodus* (Jerusalem: Elinor Library, 1976), pp. 115-118.

[4] Sandra Berg, *The Book of Esther: Motifs, Themes and Structure,* Society of Biblical Literature Dissertation Series, 44 (Missoula, Mont.: Scholars Press, 1979), p. 108.

[5] *Ibid.,* pp. 108, 109.

[6] *Ibid.,* p. 243, citing Austin M. Farrer, *St. Matthew and St. Mark* (London: Dacre Press, 1966), p. 166.

[7] Richard M. Davidson, "The Chiastic Literary Structure of the Book of Ezekiel," in *To Understand the Scriptures: Essays in Honor of William H. Shea,* ed. David Merling (Berrien Springs, Mich.: Institute of Archaeology, Andrews University, 1997), pp. 71-93.

[8] John W. Welch, ed., *Chiasmus in Antiquity* (Gerstenberg Verlag, 1981), p. 239.

[9] *Ibid.,* p. 220.

Three

GOD KNOWS EVERYTHING

Scripture well documents the prophetic role. God enlisted various men and women throughout the Old Testament period to declare His word. The prophet Jonah is but one of many. Records of such prophetic calls are a major element of the Bible.

Earlier we noticed that when God calls a prophet the biblical record lists some personal information about the individual. We find the prophets described as real people coming from places that we can identify geographically. Sometimes Scripture even specifies their families. In the case of the prophet Jonah, the author identifies him as "son of Amittai" at the very outset of the book (Jonah 1:1).

This is an important point. In our modern society not many people know us. Even among our church families we often don't know everyone. But right in the opening sentences of the book of Jonah we begin to find an amazing picture of God.

From Jonah's prophetic commission and others elsewhere in Scripture we learn that God's knowledge of each human being is remarkable. Scripture makes it clear that He is the Creator of all life. But the giving of life doesn't end His involvement with us. God is not an impersonal "cosmic force." He also sustains the vast universe that He created. Many passages in Scripture indicate this.

Psalm 104 is especially impressive in this regard. The psalm is an extended picture of God's amazing providence and care. When we read the psalm in its entirety, we discover how the divine activity follows the same order of the Genesis creation account, with one significant difference. The verbs connected with God's power are now in the present tense.

Here and in many other passages Scripture presents God in His ever-continuing role as sustainer and provider of His creation. According to the consistent testimony of the biblical writers, God did not create this world and then withdraw, leaving it to coast on its merry way alone, operating according to the natural laws that He established. Rather, we see a God who has remained vitally involved not only in nature as a whole but also in the very lives of His creatures. The picture of God in Scripture is not fuzzy, vague, or abstract.

Nor is God's knowledge of us—His human family—indefinite or even just general. Scripture informs us that God's attention to each of us is intimate and inclusive. For example, He knows details about us that we wouldn't even consider that important, such as how many hairs we each have on our heads (Matt. 10:30)! When you meet someone, is it crucial for you to know how many hairs they have on their head? No job description or government survey requests such information. But God's attention to each one of us includes what we would consider a rather minor detail.

Moreover, we don't really know someone before we have met them and have become acquainted. By contrast, God's divine cognizance of our being was intimate even before our births, as the psalmist exclaims:

"I will praise You, for I am fearfully and wonderfully made;
Marvelous are Your works,
And that my soul knows very well.
My frame was not hidden from You,
When I was made in secret,
And skillfully wrought in the lowest parts of the earth.
Your eyes saw my substance, being yet unformed.
And in Your book they all were written,
The days fashioned for me,
When as yet there were none of them" (Ps. 139:14-16).

The prophet Jeremiah speaks similarly: "Now the word of the Lord came to me saying, 'Before I formed you in the womb I knew you, and before you were born I consecrated you; I appointed you a prophet to the nations'" (Jer. 1:4, 5, NASB).

It is abundantly clear throughout Scripture that God knows each person intimately. A few examples will suffice to remind us:

1. Samuel's mother had dedicated him as a small boy to the Lord, and he served at the tabernacle under Eli at Shiloh. God called the child by name one night and trusted him with a critical message to deliver to the high priest Eli (1 Sam. 3:1-10).

2. As an adult prophet, God informed Samuel of His advance awareness of Jesse's sons and that He would choose one of them to be the future king of Israel (1 Sam. 16:1-13).

3. God knew of a widow in Zarephath that He involved in a divine miracle to provide for Elijah during a famine (1 Kings 17:8-16).

4. The Lord appoints both kings and prophets, as He instructs Elijah: "Then the Lord said to [Elijah], 'Go, return on your way to the Wilderness of Damascus; and when you arrive, anoint Hazael as king over Syria. Also you shall anoint Jehu the son of Nimshi as king over Israel. And Elisha the son of Shaphat of Abel Meholah you shall anoint as prophet in your place'" (1 Kings 19:15, 16).

5. In the New Testament, when Jesus traveled through Jericho surrounded by a crowd of people, He looked up into a sycamore tree and saw a man sitting in the branches. He didn't just call out, "Hey, you up there in the tree." Jesus spoke to the man by name: "Zacchaeus, I want to go to your house today." The tax collector was hoping just to catch a glimpse of the famous itinerant preacher, but when Jesus saw him in the branches of the tree, He referred to Zacchaeus by name (Luke 19:1-10)!

6. The apostle Paul acknowledged that God had set him apart for ministry even before his birth (Gal. 1:15).

7. God even predicted the non-Israelite ruler Cyrus by name (Isa. 44:28; 45:1). Some reject this part of the book of Isaiah as actually written in the eighth century, presuming that God could not have possibly predicted Cyrus by name so precisely hundreds of years before his birth. But we find consistent and extensive evidence throughout Scripture that God knows not only how many hairs we have on our heads, but even our names long before we are born! God Himself explicitly refers to this through Isaiah: "Fear not, [O Israel,] for I have redeemed you; *I have called you by your name*" (Isa. 43:1).

In the case of Cyrus, who wasn't even an Israelite, God insists that

He knew what his name and mission would be long before his birth. Such personal providence is one of God's notable attributes in Scripture. And it gives us a crucial insight into the type of relationship that He has with human beings. When God summons people, He never catches our attention with an impersonal "Hey, you." He knows each of us by name, even before our birth, a fact that the opening verse of the book of Jonah reminds us. God even knew Jonah's family name—the prophet was the son of Amittai.

Belief in the God of Scripture gives us personhood and purpose. Some modern philosophical movements, such as existentialism, teach that there is no God and no ultimate purpose to life. Existentialists insist that *nothing* exists outside of or beyond our own personal existence. The material world is all there is of reality. They insist that human life is meaningless, pointless, and absurd. We are alone in the universe.

But Christians who believe in Scripture know differently. Because of the extensive and consistent testimony of Scripture, we believe that there is a personal God, and that He is the Lord of heaven and earth and our Creator. He has not only given us life, but also sustains it minute by minute. "In God we live, and move, and have our being. Each heartbeat, each breath, is the inspiration of Him who breathed into the nostrils of Adam the breath of life—the inspiration of the ever-present God, the great I AM." [1] God also has a magnificent destiny for each one of us, and for that He calls us by name!

God also knows where we live. Our knowledge of world geography and even our own country may be limited. But within the pages of Scripture we find that God is not only well aware of people, but familiar with localities, cities, and nations. We regularly observe that God has precise knowledge about all people and places. Not only does He know people by name, He also knows cities by name, and is very aware of what is happening in them. The Bible gives many examples:

1. *Babel.* Humanity deliberately planned the city in defiance of God. Aware of this, God goes to it in judgment. "And they said, 'Come, let us build *for ourselves* a city . . . and let us make for ourselves a name.' . . . The Lord came down to see the city" (Gen. 11:4, 5, NASB).

40

2. *Sodom.* Nineveh was not the first city God called to judgment. God informs Abraham: "The outcry of Sodom and Gomorrah is indeed great, and their sin is exceedingly grave. . . . I will go down now" (Gen. 18:20, 21, NASB).

3. God divinely directs Jeremiah to preach to *Jerusalem* in a ministry that lasted for years as He sought to bring Judah to repentance and thus avert certain judgment against it.

4. On the occasion of Christ's baby dedication at the Temple, the prophet Anna proclaimed the birth of the Messiah to all those who were looking for redemption in the capital city of Jerusalem (Luke 2:36-38). In the original language the verb form used for Anna's proclamation implies that she did this more than once!

5. God continued to love Jerusalem. Even though it finally rejected Him, Jesus expressed deep emotion over His beloved city. "When He approached [Jerusalem], He saw the city and wept over it, saying, 'If you had known in this day, even you, the things which make for peace'" (Luke 19:41, 42).

Ellen White underscores Christ's intense affection for this city:

"When the procession reached the brow of the hill, and was about to descend into the city, Jesus halted, and all the multitude with Him. Before them lay Jerusalem in its glory, now bathed in the light of the declining sun. . . . Jesus gazes upon the scene, and the vast multitude hush their shouts, spellbound by the sudden vision of beauty. All eyes turn upon the Saviour, expecting to see in His countenance the admiration they themselves feel. But instead of this they behold a cloud of sorrow. They are surprised and disappointed to see His eyes fill with tears, and His body rock to and fro like a tree before the tempest, while a wail of anguish bursts from His quivering lips, as if from the depths of a broken heart. . . . This sudden sorrow was like a note of wailing in a grand triumphal chorus. In the midst of a scene of rejoicing, where all were paying Him homage, Israel's King was in tears; not silent tears of gladness, but tears and groans of insuppressible agony. . . . The tears of Jesus were not in anticipation of His own suffering. Just before Him was Gethsemane, where soon the horror of a great darkness would overshadow Him. . . . Nearby was Calvary, the scene of His approaching agony. Yet it was not because of these re-

41

minders of His cruel death that the Redeemer wept and groaned in anguish of spirit. His was no selfish sorrow. . . . It was the sight of Jerusalem that pierced the heart of Jesus. . . . He saw . . . what she might have been had she accepted Him who alone could heal her wound. He had come to save her; how could He give her up?"[2]

6. After the apostle Paul's dramatic conversion experience, God instructs Ananias to visit him in the city of *Damascus,* providing even the street address (Acts 9:10, 11)! When Ananias expresses concern that God might be mistaken about who Paul really was, God makes it very clear that He knows just what He is doing:

"But the Lord said to him, 'Go, for he is a chosen vessel of Mine to bear My name before Gentiles, kings, and the children of Israel. For I will show him how many things he must suffer for My name's sake'" (verses 15, 16).

7. Jonah was not the only prophet that God assigned to a city ministry. The Lord also gave travel instructions to Philip. "But an angel of the Lord spoke to Philip saying, 'Arise and go south to the road that descends from Jerusalem to Gaza'" (Acts 8:26, NASB). The Holy Spirit also summoned Peter from Joppa to Caesarea (Acts 10:19-33). Paul had an aggressive ministry in the major Gentile cities and provinces of his era, including Athens (Acys 17:16-34), Thessalonia (verses 1-4), and Corinth (Acts 18:1-11).

"As, in fulfillment of the commission given him by God, Paul had borne the gospel to the Gentiles, *he had visited many of the world's largest cities . . .*"[3]

Moreover, many of Paul's letters are linked with his public ministry to then-prominent cities, as is clear from his introductory greetings:

"Paul, an apostle . . . , to the churches of Galatia" (Gal. 1:1, 2).

"Paul, an apostle of Jesus Christ . . . , to the saints who are in Ephesus" (Eph. 1:1).

"Paul and Timothy . . . , to all the saints in Christ Jesus who are in Philippi" (Phil. 1:1).

"Paul, an apostle of Jesus Christ . . . , to the saints and faithful brethren in Christ who are in Colosse" (Col. 1:1, 2).

"Paul, . . . to the church of God which is at Corinth" opens both 1 and 2 Corinthians.

8. In the book of Revelation John receives an extensive vision linked with churches in seven cities (Rev. 2; 3).

Ellen White, who spoke often and clearly about the importance of country living for rearing children, wrote just as intensely about God's concern for the major cities of the world.

"Wake up, wake up, my brethren and sisters, and enter the fields in America that have never been worked. After you have given something for foreign fields, do not think your duty done. There is a work to be done in foreign fields, but there is a work to be done in America that is just as important. In the cities of America there are people of almost every language. These need the light that God has given to His church." [4]

"In New York City, in Chicago, and in other great centers of population, there is a larger foreign element—multitudes of various nationalities, and all practically unwarned. Among Seventh-day Adventists there is a great zeal—and I am not saying there is any too much—to work in foreign countries; but it would be pleasing to God if a proportionate zeal were manifested to work the cities close by. His people need to move sensibly. They need to set about this work in the cities with serious earnestness. Men of consecration and talent are to be sent into these cities and set to work. Many classes of laborers are to unite in conducting these efforts to warn the people." [5]

"There is no change in the messages that God has sent in the past. The work in the cities is the essential work for this time. When the cities are worked as God would have them, the result will be the setting in operation of a mighty movement such as we have not yet witnessed." [6]

"The cause of God in the earth today is in need of living representatives of Bible truth. The ordained ministers alone are not equal to the task of warning the great cities. God is calling not only upon ministers, but also upon physicians, nurses, colporteurs, Bible workers, and other consecrated laymen of varied talent who have a knowledge of the Word of God and who know the power of His grace, to consider the needs of the unwarned cities. Time is rapidly passing, and there is much to be done. Every agency must be set in operation, that present opportunities may be wisely improved." [7]

"The lesson is for God's messengers today, when the cities of the nations are as verily in need of a knowledge of the attributes and purposes of the true God as were the Ninevites of old. . . . The only city that will endure is the city whose builder and maker is God. . . . The Lord Jesus is calling upon men to strive with sanctified ambition to secure the immortal inheritance."[8]

Thus we should not be surprised with God's concern about a major city of Jonah's day, when He pointedly directs Jonah's steps to the capital city of Assyria. Nineveh was an ancient and populous city on the fertile banks of the Tigris founded by Asshur, who left the land of Shinar about the time of Babel's dispersion.[9] The first scriptural mention of Nineveh occurs long before the book of Jonah. Genesis 10:8-11 informs that it was connected with "Nimrod the mighty hunter." Ellen White describes its prominence in the time of Jonah: "Among the cities of the ancient world in the days of divided Israel one of the greatest was Nineveh, the capital of the Assyrian realm."[10]

Archaeologists have excavated the main outline of the walls of the ancient city of Nineveh that Jonah likely saw. The chief palace in existence when God sent him to preach to Nineveh was probably that of Ashurnasirpal, a king whose name means "the god Assur is guardian of the heir." If so, Jonah would have probably been summoned to it to deliver his judgment message some 60-100 years after its construction. The buildings alone occupied six acres.

Diodorus Siculus of the first century B.C. describes Nineveh as a quadrangle, measuring 150 stadia by 90, with a total perimeter of 480 stadia, or about 60 miles. This agrees favorably with the record of Nineveh in the book of Jonah as a "city of three days' journey" (Jonah 3:3, KJV).

In view of Jonah's experience with the "great fish," it is particularly interesting to note that the Hebrew "Nineweh" is a translation of the Assyrian "Ninua." This in turn is a rendering of the earlier Sumerian "Nina." Nina was a name of the goddess Ishtar, represented as a fish inside a womb.

Nineveh was about 500 miles to the northeast of Israel. To obey God's commission, Jonah would have had to make a tremendous journey across the desert on foot or camel train. And all this meant making extensive effort to travel to the capital city of one of Israel's looming enemies. God knew the name of Assyria's capital city. He also was aware that Nineveh was no obscure village, for He describes it as a "great city" (Jonah 1:2). Later on the prophet himself will admit he was well aware of its reputation as an idolatrous, sin-ridden city (Jonah 4:2).

The word "great" is one of the most repeated words in the book of Jonah. Though it occurs a total of 38 times in all the other minor prophets combined, it appears eight times in just four chapters of Jonah, describing not only the "great city" of Nineveh (Jonah 1:2; 3:2, 3; 4:11), but also the "great wind" (Jonah 1:4), the "great tempest" (verse 12), and the "great fish" (verse 17).

Here is a good place to remind ourselves that when we find certain words repeated in a biblical narrative, those words become key pointers to trigger our thinking as we read. The writer is seeking to underscore something, deliberately restricting his vocabulary to do so. Numerous times in the book of Jonah the biblical writer uses the word "great" to describe Nineveh or the Ninevites. Its usage specifies and stresses the importance of the city, intensifying to "an exceedingly great city" in the third chapter. Thus the book gets the point across: Nineveh is no small insignificant hamlet. And God's concerns correspond.

The narrative text also makes clear that God was aware of the bustling metropolis's moral standing. He specifically informs Jonah that "their wickedness has come up before Me" (Jonah 1:2). Nineveh has had a long time of grace and forbearance. The Lord at last sits down at His tribunal, ready to judge Nineveh's case. The city is intolerably "wicked," and God Himself has convened the case. The cutting knife of divine morality flashes from God's throne to the "great" but ethically dark capital city of Nineveh. God has an unmistakable judgment message for one of the chief cities of the Gentile world at that time.

Though Nineveh was a stronghold of pagan glory, God also reveals that He is fully aware of its violence and wickedness. Later the Lord will send yet another prophet, Nahum, to again confront the citizens of Nineveh with their wickedness. The book of Nahum includes graphic detail of the terrible evil found there. The combined ministries of the two prophets reminds us how much attention God invested in this preeminent city.

Yes, in Scripture we always find God deeply involved with individual people. He knows intimate details of their lives and hearts. But His omniscience includes much more. God is also aware of the moral caliber of major population centers. And He cares.

* * * * * * * *

Soliloquy of a City Shepherd

God is the God of the cities. And I am His shepherd to the city . . .
my mission—main street!
I walk with God in fields of asphalt
where the flowers are the weeds of
wasted men.
I move among the mountains of mortar
in metropolis . . .
in the valley of the living dead
entombed in tall walls of skyscraper sepulchers.
I mingle among the milling myriads . . .
going everywhere . . .
going nowhere . . .
I hear the sound of the city . . .
hear the cruel cacophony of caterpillar
and human cry . . .
hear the dying deliberations of the
disillusioned
in the peoples' parliament of pain.
I know the sound of the city . . .
know the incredible contradiction of
angel song and serpent hiss . . .
in the sound of the city.
I feel the pulse of the city . . .
feel the motion, the movement of the
mighty metropolis . . .
and I thrill and I chill
at the eerie awe of the city's confused
cadence.
I see the city . . .
stand in stunned silence before
the aristocracy of stone and steel.

I see the city's stately structures
glistening in sun-kissed glory at midday . . .
only to know that at midnight that
sacred skyline
shall become a symbol of shame in silhouette.
I watch the machine in the name of
renewal plow up the people
and push the broken plans of broken men
into the dumping ground of the deserted . . .
and I know that the land, not man, is
renewed . . .
that the elegant architecture that
rises there
stands in unmitigated mockery of the
men
who were moved out to make room
for its marble majesty.
I know the ills of inner urbia . . .
know of the pushers, the apostles of
poison . . .
the architects of the addict's anguish . . .
know that under the shadow of steeple and tower
these harpies of hell
spawn their sad sons of the needle.
I know of the good in the city . . .
know of the many who minister
mercy
to the men of sin in the city . . .
and I wonder how so much good
can reach so far and touch so few.
I weep for my city . . .
weep for the evil and ill of urbia . . .
and I remember him who wept over
the sacred city . . .
remember that it was he who sent
me to the city . . .

sent me to weep
sent me to love and lift and lead.
And I know I need not pray:
"Lord, go before me
through these lonely lanes of the
millions" . . .
for I know that over every
aching acre of asphalt
His Spirit has moved in mercy . . .
that every single stepping-stone has
felt
the tender touch of His sacred sandal.
I am shepherd to the city . . .
my mission—mercy . . .
mercy to the multitudes of
metropolis!"
—Francis Marquis Debose, superintendent of missions, Detroit
(*Home Missions,* September 1965, pp. 6, 7).[11]

[1] Ellen G. White, *Medical Ministry* (Mountain View, Calif.: Pacific Press Pub. Assn., 1932), p. 9.

[2] White, *The Desire of Ages* (Mountain View, Calif.: Pacific Press Pub. Assn., 1898), pp. 575, 576.

[3] White, *The Acts of the Apostles* (Mountain View, Calif.: Pacific Press Pub. Assn., 1911), p. 406. (Italics supplied.)

[4] White, *Testimonies for the Church* (Mountain View, Calif.: Pacific Press Pub. Assn., 1948), vol. 8, p. 36.

[5] White, *Christian Service* (Washington, D.C.: General Conference of Seventh-day Adventists, 1947), p. 199.

[6] White, *Medical Ministry,* p. 304.

[7] White, *The Acts of the Apostles,* p. 158.

[8] White, *Conflict and Courage* (Washington, D.C.: Review and Herald Pub. Assn., 1970), p. 230.

[9] White, in *Review and Herald,* Oct. 18, 1906.

[10] White, *Prophets and Kings* (Mountain View, Calif.: Pacific Press Pub. Assn., 1917), p. 265.

[11] Roland Hegstad, former editor of *Liberty* magazine and now editor of *Perspective Digest,* presented this poem in a sermon for the Adventist Theological Society in Toronto, Canada, and graciously shared with me a copy. I have been unable to locate any address for the author or copyright holder.

GOD IS
A JUDGE

The narrative continues. God has personally conferred the prophetic task on Jonah. From an additional reference to Jonah in 2 Kings 14:25 we learn where he lived and that he was God's mouth-piece more than once: "according to the word of the Lord God of Israel, which He had spoken through His servant Jonah the son of Amittai, the prophet who was from Gath Hepher." Gath Hepher is just a few miles north of Nazareth in the region of lower Galilee, making Jonah a prophet of the northern kingdom. Thus Jonah's life is well documented intertextually.

We also discover at the very opening of the book that God is well aware of the "great city" of Nineveh and its moral degradation. He instructs Jonah to "cry out against it; for their wickedness have come up before Me" (Jonah 1:2).

Archaeologists have excavated and translated numerous ancient Assyrian inscriptions. For example, the following document comes from the reign of Ashurnasirpal II (884-859 B.C.). It alone reminds us how accurate God was in His evaluation of the Assyrians. The monarch boasts:

"I built a pillar over against his city and I flayed all the chiefs who had revolted, and covered the pillar with their skin. Some I walled up within the pillar, some I impaled upon the pillar on stakes, and others I bound to stakes round about the pillar . . . and cut the limbs of the officers, of the royal officers who had rebelled. . . .

"Many captives from among them I burned with fire, and many I took as living captives. From some I cut off their noses, their ears and their fingers; of many I put out the eyes. I made one pillar of the living

49

and another of heads, and I bound their heads to tree trunks round about the city. Their young men and maidens I burned in the fire.

"Twenty men I captured alive and I immured them in the wall of his palace. . . . The rest of their warriors I consumed with thirst in the desert of the Euphrates."[1]

Along with many such ancient inscriptions, exquisitely carved granite wall panels also portray graphically the legendary Assyrian cruelty that God referred to. Assyrian civilization had a widespread reputation for violence. God had rightly indicted its capital city. As we recalled in the last chapter, the Lord even commissioned another prophet, Nahum, to condemn the wickedness of Nineveh. Listen to the divine accusation:

"The burden against Nineveh. The book of the vision of Nahum
the Elkoshite. . . .
The Lord has given a command concerning you:
'Your name shall be perpetuated no longer.
Out of the house of your gods
I will cut off the carved image and the molded image.
I will dig your grave,
For you are vile.' . . .
Woe to the *bloody city!*
It is all full of lies and robbery.
Its victim never departs. . . .
There is a multitude of slain,
A great number of bodies,
Countless corpses—
They stumble over the corpses—
Because of the multitude of harlotries of the seductive harlot,
The mistress of sorceries,
Who sells nations through her harlotries,
And families through her sorceries.
'Behold, I am against you,' says the Lord of hosts. . . .
'Your injury has no healing,
Your wound is severe.
All who hear news of you
Will clap their hands over you,

For *upon whom has not your wickedness passed continually?'"* (Nahum 1:1–3:19).

A striking aspect of the double ministry of Jonah and Nahum to the Assyrian capital of Nineveh is God's pointed concern about the city. This aspect deserves serious consideration. Have our own hearts ever stirred for the major cities of our world, filled as they are with corruption? Have we really ever yearned for the inhabitants of such vast metropolises in the same way that Scripture tells us that the heart of God does? Sometimes, after noting the various news reports of the depravity perpetuated in many of them, we may have even mused that if they suffer some major disaster they are only getting what they deserve.

In the scriptural record we find God fully cognizant of the wickedness in Babel, Sodom and Gomorrah, Corinth, and Rome. He never ignores their fate. And that is just what we find in the book of Jonah.

Divine judgment troubles some Christians, however. It disturbs them that God judges wickedness. It is hard for some to believe that a God of love can also be a God of judgment. Yet, the biblical picture of God reveals just that.

The Lord's command to Jonah about Nineveh should not surprise us. It was grounded in God's consistent standard of righteousness and justice against sin, a fact that He states plainly to Jonah: "their wickedness has come up before Me."

This is clearly legal language. The Lord, speaking as a judge, is announcing Nineveh's indictment. Never mind the many modern voices that seek to soothe our consciences with an almost exclusive focus on divine love. We observe here and all through Scripture that God notices human wickedness. Thus it is a most serious moment for Nineveh.

In the short book of Jonah the word "evil" appears 10 times and as both noun and verb. As we have already stressed, when doing sensitive narrative analysis in Scripture we must take careful notice of the choice of words and their repetitions. Biblical writers did not use modern techniques of emphasis such as underlining or italics. Instead, they carefully selected their vocabulary in light of what they intended to communicate and emphasize. Within its four chapters the book of Jonah used the word "evil" more than once to refer to the Ninevites. The reader is to understand that the city of Nineveh is not a peaceful hamlet and that its wickedness and violence has not gone unnoticed in heaven.

We also learn in Scripture that God never plays favorites. Nor does He administer judgment unfairly. God often confronted the nation of Israel with His absolute and unvarying moral standard and issued solemn calls to judgment when necessary. For example:

"The word of the Lord came to me: . . . thus says the Lord God to the land of Israel: An end! The end has come upon the four corners of the land. Now the end is upon you, I will let loose my anger upon you; I will judge you according to your ways, I will punish you for all your abominations. My eye will not spare you, I will have no pity. I will punish you for your ways, while your abominations are among you. Then you shall know that I am the Lord" (Eze. 7:1-4, NRSV).

As we noted earlier, God directed other prophets such as Isaiah and Jeremiah to issue divine warnings to nations outside of Israel.[2] Long before Israel was a nation God had held ancient rulers accountable to the same moral standard as those in the covenant line. It is imperative to understand that the divine standard of morality was operative even before God gave the Decalogue on Sinai. The Ten Commandments have always been in effect! Let us review the evidence for this important point.

In Genesis 12 Abraham traveled to Egypt because of a famine. He persuaded his wife, Sarah, to lie about their relationship. Abraham's hunch that Pharaoh would want to have Sarah as a wife was right, and the Egyptian ruler took her. But God Himself brought judgment on Pharaoh. However, the Egyptian ruler was distressed that he had been lied to.

"But the Lord plagued Pharaoh and his house with great plagues because of Sarai, Abram's wife. And Pharaoh called Abram and said, 'What is this you have done to me? Why did you not tell me that she was your wife? Why did you say, "She is my sister"? I might have taken her as my wife. Now therefore, here is your wife; take her and go your way'" (Gen. 12:17-19).

Later, in a similar situation, Abraham again lied. Again God intervened, and again the ruler, this time of Gerar, also exhibited an obvious standard of morality. "But God came to Abimelech in a dream by night, and said to him, 'Indeed you are a dead man because of the woman whom you have taken, for she is a man's wife.' But Abimelech had not come near her, and he said, 'Lord, will You slay a righteous nation also? Did he not say to me, "She is my sister"? And she, even she herself said, "He is my brother." In the integrity of my heart and innocence of my hands I have done this.' And God said to him in a dream, 'Yes, I know that you did this in the integrity of your heart. For I also withheld you from sinning against Me; therefore I did not let you touch her. Now therefore, restore the man's wife' " (Gen. 20:3-7).

God did not destroy the cities of Sodom and Gomorrah simply because He was feeling miffed. Nor was He arbitrarily irritated, as the Near Eastern gods could be. Again the reason is clear: "And the Lord said, 'Because the outcry against Sodom and Gomorrah is great, and because their sin is very grave' " (Gen. 18:20).

The two angels repeat the same indictment to Lot: "Have you anyone else here? . . . Take them out of this place! For we will destroy this place, because the outcry against them has grown great before the face of the Lord, and the Lord has sent us to destroy it" (Gen. 19:12, 13).

Joseph's response to Potiphar's seductive wife is also instructive: "'There is no one greater in this house than I, nor has he [Potiphar] kept anything from me but you, because you are his wife. *How then can I do this great wickedness, and sin against God?"* (Gen. 39:9). Joseph could have argued that he did not want to dishonor Potiphar. However, he appealed to a higher authority.

The book of Job is recognized as the oldest book in the Old Testament. Notably, Job is not of the covenant line. He lived before the great Exodus deliverance of the Israelites, yet he too exhibits a high standard of morality. In Job 31 he comments specifically on lying (verses 5, 6); covetousness (verses 7, 8); adultery (verses 9-12); idolatry (verses 24-28); stealing (verses 38-40); and caring for the poor and exhibiting social justice (verses 16-23).

Even more important, God made it very clear why He brought final judgment to the antediluvians and destroyed the world by a flood: "Then the Lord saw that the wickedness of man was great in the earth, and that every intent of the thoughts of his heart was only evil continually" (Gen. 6:5).

All through Scripture, beginning in Genesis and climaxing in Revelation, we find God absolutely consistent in His standard of justice. He judged the moral failures of Israel as well as those of all other nations. Not only did Jonah and Nahum call Assyria to judgment, but also Isaiah, as we have seen:

"Therefore it shall come to pass, when the Lord has performed all His work on Mount Zion and on Jerusalem, that He will say, 'I will punish the fruit of the arrogant heart of the king of Assyria, and the glory of his haughty looks.' For he says: 'By the strength of my hand I have done it, and by my wisdom, for I am prudent; also I have removed the boundaries of the people, and have robbed their treasuries; so I have put down the inhabitants like a valiant man' " (Isa. 10:12, 13).

The prophet Amos, living in the same century as Jonah, also delivered strong indictments against sin to nations beyond Israel:

" 'The Lord roars from Zion,
And utters His voice from Jerusalem;
The pastures of the shepherds mourn,
And the top of Carmel withers.'
Thus says the Lord:
'For three transgressions of Damascus, and for four,
I will not turn away its punishment.' . . .
'For three transgressions of Gaza, and for four,
I will not turn away its punishment,
Because they took captive the whole captivity
To deliver them up to Edom' " (Amos 1:2-6).

However, much modern thinking considers divine judgment irreconcilable with a God of love. Regarding judgment an outdated concept since the death of Christ, many Christians think that our focus should now be exclusively on God's love. However, in the minds of biblical writers this dichotomy between love and justice simply did not exist. For them, when God cries for justice, His call issues from His heart of love, as Fleming Rutledge so eloquently states:

"The Bible shows us in a thousand different ways that God's judgment is *an instrument of* his mercy. Judgment does not mean everlasting condemnation . . . ; it means a course correction in the direction of salvation. Wise parents have always known this."[3]

Ellen White concurs and comments pointedly on this issue many times. For example, as she describes God's punishment of Israel after the rebellion at Sinai, she includes numerous reasons why it had to be done:

"*Love no less than justice* demanded that for this sin judgment should be inflicted. God is the guardian as well as the sovereign of His people. *He cuts off those who are determined upon rebellion, that they may not lead others to ruin.* In sparing the life of Cain, God had demonstrated to the universe what would be the result of permitting sin to go unpunished. The influence exerted upon his descendants by his life and teaching led to the state of corruption that demanded the destruction of the whole world by a flood. *The history of the antediluvians testifies that long life is not a blessing to the sinner; God's great forbearance did not repress their wickedness. The longer men lived, the more corrupt they became.*

"So with the *apostasy at Sinai. Unless punishment had been speedily visited upon transgression, the same results would again have been seen. The earth would have become as corrupt as in the days of Noah.* Had these transgressors been spared, evils would have followed, greater than resulted from sparing the life of Cain. It was the *mercy of God* that thousands should suffer, to prevent the necessity of visiting judgments upon millions. In order to save the many, He must punish the few. Furthermore, *as the people had cast off their allegiance to God, they had forfeited the divine protection, and, deprived of their defense, the whole nation was exposed to the power of their enemies. Had not the evil been promptly put away, they would soon have fallen a prey to their numerous and powerful foes.* It was *necessary for the good of Israel,* and also as a *lesson to all succeeding generations,* that crime should be promptly punished. And it was *no less a mercy to the sinners themselves that they should be cut short in their evil course.* Had their life been spared, the same spirit that led them to rebel against God would have been manifested in hatred and strife among themselves, and they would eventually have destroyed one another. *It was in love to the world, in love to Israel, and even to the transgressors, that crime was punished with swift and terrible severity.*"[4]

God's moral involvement in the nations of the world surely was not an unknown concept to Jonah. But it is easy to become blind to God's perspective on sin. No person is immune to the danger. Nor were Jonah and Israel overjoyed that God could extend His mercy beyond their national boundaries. Both overlooked how God had always expressed His concern for all humanity. Even the ancient Noahic and Abrahamic covenants pointedly included all people. Jonah and his people forgot how God had earlier prepared a "deliverer" during a great famine to bring relief not only to Egypt but the surrounding nations, including Jacob and his sons (Gen. 45:7, 8). Now God needed to remind them how He had always included "foreigners" within His mercy. Even Naaman, a Syrian army commander and thus potential national enemy, had been healed of his leprosy in Israel. Many of the Israelite prophets even speak of God's intentions to bless the whole world:

"Thus says the Lord: Maintain justice, and do what is right, for soon my salvation will come, and my deliverance be revealed. . . . And the foreigners who join themselves to the Lord, to minister to him, to love the name of the Lord, and to be his servants, all who keep the sabbath, and do not profane it, and hold fast my covenant—these I will bring to my holy mountain, and make them joyful in my house of prayer; their burnt offerings and their sacrifices will be accepted on my altar; for my house shall be called a house of prayer for all peoples" (Isa. 56:1-7, NRSV).

We too must be honest enough to admit to ourselves that it is easy to lack concern for or even become prejudiced against another people group or nation. During New Testament times Simon Peter, son of a later Jonah, struggled with the same issues as did the Old Testament prophet Jonah. And in the same town of Joppa! Recall what God declares to Peter: " 'What God has cleansed you must not call common.' This was done three times" (Acts 10:15, 16).

Since we are training ourselves to become more sensitive to narrative writing in Scripture, the threefold repetition of the divine admonition should jump out at us! Peter's own explanation of his vision makes it clear that he realized that it did not involve proper dietary habits, but instead revealed God's compassion for all people:

"Then he said to them, 'You know how unlawful it is for a Jewish man to keep company with or go to one of another nation. But God has shown me that I should not call any man common or unclean.' . . . 'In truth I perceive that God shows no partiality. But in every nation whoever fears Him and works righteousness is accepted by Him'" (verses 28-35).

God knows all people and all places by name. He knows the minutest details of our outward physical appearance. Even more important, He knows what lurks in the depths of our hearts, including those areas we have been able to disguise and cover up from anyone else—and often even ourselves. God also demonstrates such intimate personal concern on a global scale. And His standard of morality is clear and consistent in both Testaments, as we have seen:

"O Lord, how great are Your works!
Your thoughts are very deep.
A senseless man does not know,
Nor does a fool understand this.
When the wicked spring up like grass,
And when all the workers of iniquity flourish,
It is that they may be destroyed forever.
But You, Lord, are on high forevermore.
For behold, Your enemies, O Lord,
For behold, Your enemies shall perish;
All the workers of iniquity shall be scattered" (Ps. 92:5-9).

In light of all this, it should not surprise us that God enlists Jonah to pronounce doom on Nineveh's wickedness. Who would have thought that God had anything but judgment in store for the wicked city of Nineveh? Violence can bring down the mightiest nations. However, though divine judgment is certain, it is not the last divine word for Nineveh! God's judgment call to Nineveh should remind us that we can't often predict what He will do. No one can ever presume to know what God is going to do next. The next detail in His master plan may surprise us.

For example, who of Joseph's brothers would have believed that he would someday be prime minister in Egypt? But Joseph testified to God's personal involvement in his life:

"Then Joseph said to his brothers, 'Please come closer to me.' And they came closer. And he said, 'I am your brother Joseph, whom you sold into Egypt. Now do not be grieved or angry with yourselves, because you sold me here, for God sent me before you to preserve life. . . . *God sent me before you* to preserve for you a remnant in the earth, and to keep you alive by a great deliverance. Now, *therefore, it was not you who sent me here, but God*'" (Gen. 45:4-8, NASB). Two times in this one passage Joseph pointedly repeats that God's providence was directly involved in his being in Egypt.

Who would have dreamed that four teenage Hebrew prisoners of war would rise to such political prominence in the land of their captivity, Babylon? Who would have thought that God would enlist a herdsman of Tekoa to pronounce a judgment on Israel and the surrounding nations (Amos 1)? Who in the early church would have thought that someone like Saul of Tarsus would be converted? And who would have even suggested that anyone should pray for his conversion? Even the prophet Ananias trembled at God's instructions to visit Saul in Damascus:

"Then Ananias answered, 'Lord, I have heard from many about this man, how much harm he has done to Your saints in Jerusalem. And here he has authority from the chief priests to bind all who call on Your name'" (Acts 9:13, 14).

God surely surprised Jonah too when He dispatched the prophet to a Gentile city—one of the most infamous pagan cities then on the face of the earth. And on top of that, God was breaking all normal precedents with Jonah's mission. He alone of all God's prophets ever received such a commission. The Lord did something astonishing and glorious when He appointed a prophet to travel beyond the boundaries of Israel. God violated all the current Israelite notions of prophetic ministry by dispatching His first "apostle" to the Gentiles!

However, Jonah seemed to prefer that God should funnel His mercy exclusively on the Israelites. After all, he later admits, the wicked Ninevites justly deserved to suffer the penalty for their sins.

As we will see, Jonah admits to God that he was well aware of Nineveh's reputation as an idolatrous, sin-ridden city (Jonah 4:2). And we will observe through the prophet's actions that apparently nothing was more repulsive or repugnant or distressing to him than going there to preach repentance. Nineveh, the center of Assyrian power, was the capital city of Israel's worst enemy. Once again Assyria was looming as a threat to Israel's security and survival. The drama of the situation is profound as a clash of wills begins with God's command to Jonah to go to Nineveh.

But before we are too harsh on Jonah, we need to ask ourselves: Have we ever noticed someone and thought of them as beyond the possibility of conversion and a waste of time to try to help them? Have we ever admitted to ourselves that we are a bit reluctant to share with others God's final judgment message? Are there some people that we would rather avoid?

God's judgment message to Nineveh includes yet another surprise. This moment of judgment for Nineveh also implies His mercy. Yes, the people of Nineveh were notoriously wicked, and He commissioned Jonah to bring Nineveh a judgment message. However, they could be thankful for that. Though often hard to recognize at the time, a judgment message from God actually is a sign of His great mercy. The greatest curse that can ever threaten a nation or a people is not to be called to judgment, but rather for God to turn away. This happened even with His own people: "Ephraim is joined to idols, *let him alone*" (Hosea 4:17). Paul reminds us again of the same issue in Romans: "And even as they did not like to retain God in their knowledge, *God gave them over* to a debased mind" (Rom. 1:28).

When people have determinably refused God, He finally has no choice but reluctantly to turn away. He gives them over to a reprobate mind—a perverse mind that cannot grasp truth. Judgment is an extremely serious matter for heaven. Thus this was a critical time for Nineveh. But it would have been even worse if God had just abandoned them without issuing a warning of impending judgment. Yes, ultimately He had to reject Nineveh. But before He did, He first sent two prophets to the great city.

God's mercy to Nineveh is just the beginning of the astonishing features in the book of Jonah. We have already noted Him calling Jonah by name and entrusting an Israelite prophet with a judgment message, a familiar Old Testament pattern. Thus we would expect that Jonah's response to the call of God would be the same as that of other prophets. But what happens next is far from routine. The book of Jonah upsets any conventional notions about God's servants. Instead, to our surprise, we find Jonah rejecting his divine mission. In fact, the book of Jonah, and indeed the entire Bible, does not present an epic tale of the human search for God. Instead we find Him doing the seeking. And many of His children, like Jonah, are reluctant to let Him do so. As James Edwards notes:

"The God of the Bible does not draw intrepid souls upward to the Olympian heights. Nor can God be found by concentrating our powers and plumbing the depths within. God does something far more unsettling: he breaks into this world, even when he is unexpected and unwelcome. God joins us in our weakest and worst moments."[5]

Other surprises will also unfold throughout the book of Jonah as we continue our "close reading of the text."

---

[1] D. D. Luckenbill, *Ancient Records of Assyria and Babylonia* (Ancient Records Series 1), cited in Geoffrey T. Bull, *The City and the Sign: An Interpretation of the Book of Jonah* (London: Hodder and Stoughton, 1970).

[2] Isaiah: Babylon (Isa. 13); Assyria (Isa. 14:24-27); Philistia (Isa. 14:28-32); Moab (Isa. 15; 16); Damascus (Isa. 17); Ethiopia (Isa. 18); Egypt (Isa. 19; 20); and Tyre (Isa. 23). Jeremiah: Babylon (Jer. 25:12-38; 50; 51); Philistia (Jer. 47); Moab (Jer. 48); Ammon (Jer. 49:1-6); Edom (verses 7-22); Damascus (Jer. 49:23-27); Kedar and Hazor (verses 28-33); and Elam (verses 34-39).

[3] Fleming Rutledge, *Help My Unbelief* (Grand Rapids: Eerdmans, 2000), p. 60.

[4] E. G. White, *Patriarchs and Prophets* (Mountain View, Calif.: Pacific Press Pub. Assn., 1890), pp. 324-326. (Italics supplied.)

[5] James R. Edwards, *The Divine Intruder: When God Breaks Into Your Life* (Colorado Springs, Colo.: NavPress, 2000), p. 17.

Five

THE GREAT ESCAPE

Thus far, the narrative in the book of Jonah has presented a recognizable situation in Scripture—that of a prophet receiving a divine call. What happens next in the Jonah narrative, however, is not the expected response: "But Jonah arose to flee to Tarshish from the presence of the Lord" (Jonah 1:3). The biblical writer then gives a detailed description of what Jonah did to escape his divine directive. It reminds us that it is one thing to profess belief in God and quite another to be able to accept His call to perform an unwelcome task!

Careful narrative analysis alerts us to the concentration of verbs used in just a single verse to describe Jonah's behavior (verse 3, KJV):

* he *rose up* to flee (employing the same verb God had used when He instructed Jonah to "arise" in verse 1)
* he *went down* to Joppa
* he *found* a ship
* he *paid* the fare
* he *went down* into it

All this flurry of activity by Jonah just for the express purpose of evading a divine command. In biblical narratives the pace of activity is an important detail to notice. The author accomplishes this through a sudden dense concentration of verbs, or an unbroken chain of verbs attached to a single person or subject. In narrative writing it indicates some particular emphasis or single-minded purpose. Other biblical examples include the description of Rebekah making the preparations for Jacob to deceive Isaac. Notice the cluster of verbs in Genesis 27:15-17. Likewise, we encounter a concentration of verbs when Abraham prepares for the sacrifice of Isaac on Mount Moriah (Gen.

22:9, 10) and when David battles Goliath (1 Sam. 17:48-51). We could cite hundreds of other examples, for it is a distinctive feature of narrative writing.

Jonah's negative response, stressed by a cluster of verbs, is not the only time in Scripture that we observe a person initially shrinking from their divinely commissioned task. Some did respond in exemplary ways, such as Mary's attitude of humility and trust at the angel Gabriel's announcement to her: "Behold the maidservant of the Lord! Let it be to me according to your word" (Luke 1:38). Others, however, were more reluctant. When God directed Moses to return to Egypt to lead the Israelites out of slavery, he was at first very hesitant, "overwhelmed by the thought of the strange and wonderful work before him."[1] He told God: "But suppose they will not believe me or listen to my voice; suppose they say, 'The Lord has not appeared to you.'. . . 'O my Lord, I am not eloquent, neither before nor since You have spoken to Your servant; but I am slow of speech and slow of tongue.'. . . 'O my Lord, please send by the hand of whomever else You may send'" (Ex. 4:1-13). God spent some time assuaging Moses' doubts, as the lengthy dialogue in Exodus 4 records. But Moses ultimately did accept the challenge.

"The divine command given to Moses found him self-distrustful, slow of speech, and timid. He was overwhelmed with a sense of his incapacity to be a mouthpiece for God to Israel. But having once accepted the work, he entered upon it with his whole heart, putting all his trust in the Lord. The greatness of his mission called into exercise the best powers of his mind. God blessed his ready obedience, and he became eloquent, hopeful, self-possessed, and well fitted for the greatest work ever given to man."[2]

Centuries later the nation of Israel splintered. The northern kingdom fell first through apostasy. The situation in Jerusalem and Judah deteriorated, and God called Jeremiah to warn the Israelites in the hope that they might repent and return to God and avoid exile. Again, the task was daunting. And Jeremiah also initially resisted God's bidding: "Then said I: 'Ah, Lord God! Behold, I cannot speak, for I am a youth'" (Jer. 1:6).

Yes, both Moses and Jeremiah shrank from their divine assignments at the outset, but from feelings of personal inadequacy. Jonah's blunt refusal goes far beyond their initial hesitation. As James Edwards observes, "Abraham, Moses, and Gideon may dialogue with God, and Jacob may even contend with God, but not Jonah. Jonah short-circuits the whole process; when God speaks, he takes to his heels."[3]

The narrator seems to hint at what might have been churning in Jonah's mind in his determination to escape God's call. In a single verse, as we saw earlier, the reader finds a double statement of the phrase that Jonah fled "from the presence of the Lord."

A single inclusion of the phrase would be a big enough shock. However, its duplication in just one verse compels us to wonder what Jonah might have been thinking. For, as we have already noted, duplication or repetition of words or a phrase serves as one method that biblical narrative writers employ to emphasize a point. In this case, the repetition alerts the reader to the irony of anyone, let alone a prophet, thinking they can escape the Lord's presence.

Intertextual links draw us back to the first time the phrase "from the presence of the Lord" appears in Scripture. Following an amazing conversation between God and the first murderer immediately after he had killed his brother, Scripture declares that "Cain went out *from the presence of the Lord* and dwelt in the land of Nod on the east of Eden" (Gen. 4:16).

Christians who believe that God is the ultimate author of the Bible understand that such intertextuality reflects the unity of thought that "cements" all Scripture together. It also informs our understanding of the nuances of meaning reflected in the recurring vocabulary and phrases of Scripture. In the case of Jonah the prophet deliberately rejected God's instructions to him.

Notice that Jonah didn't just merely leave. Rather, he *"fled."* And as we noted earlier, the verse even mentions three times the destination of the ticket Jonah purchased.

Hebrew narratives do not usually describe the thought processes of the main characters. In this case, the biblical author does not tell explicitly what Jonah was thinking about. Instead, he repeats a key phrase and depicts the prophet's actions through a verb cluster, which help provide clues as to what might have been in Jonah's mind as he arranged his passage on the ship. Perhaps he hoped to delay the implementing of God's directions in case God just might change His mind. Later, when we come to chapter 4 in the book, the prophet will admit some of his negative thinking. In the meantime, Ellen White instructs us that as Jonah "thought of the difficulties and seeming impossibilities of this commission, he was tempted to question the wisdom of the call." He brooded about what "could be gained by proclaiming such a message in that proud city."[4]

Does this attitude sound familiar? Can we identify with it? Have we ever been uneasy about the "difficulties and seeming impossibilities" of the instructions that God has given us? Have we ever run in the opposite direction from where He is calling? Do we ever hope that God might change His mind about what He is asking us to do?

Some Christians today claim that God actually matures in His thinking. Called "process theology," the theory argues that God grows and matures just as we human beings do. He is not omniscient or all-powerful. Instead He is "open" to the future and merely part of history's unfolding events. Its proponents theorize that God's mind improves as it "processes" what happens in the world. As He watches what transpires in human history it enriches and transforms His thinking. His dealing with human nature through the centuries helps Him to develop better ways of administering His kingdom. God grows in His thinking—just as we do!

This theory allows the possibility that God can speak in conflicting terms, even contradicting Himself in different periods of history, for He is only in the "process" of learning and developing better methods to manage His universe. Unfortunately, such thinking can lead, among other things, to the concept that there can be no absolutes or eternal principles, for the simple reason that even God continues to learn and improve.

However, the picture we find of God in the book of Jonah and all through Scripture strongly contradicts such a perspective. The book of Jonah itself reveals to us just how determined He is to get His message to Nineveh. He doesn't change His mind about His concern for the pagan capital city or even whom He selected as His messenger, never mind that Jonah chooses to disobey Him. God knows what He is doing. Humans may be fickle and always maturing, but God is not.

Many biblical examples reveal this picture of God, such as that of Persian ruler Cyrus and the three weeks of intense attention that heaven pours on him (Isa. 44:28; Dan. 10:13; notice that the divine intervention resumes in verse 20). And we must not overlook Christ's great struggle in Gethsemane. There He collapsed prostrate on the cold earth:

"He felt that by sin He was being separated from His Father. The gulf was so broad, so black, so deep, that His spirit shuddered before it. This agony He must not exert his divine power to escape. As man He must suffer the consequences of man's sin. As man He must endure the wrath of God against transgression. . . . He feared that in His human nature He would be unable to endure the coming conflict with the powers of darkness. . . . The conflict was terrible. . . . Behold Him contemplating the price to be paid for the human soul. In His agony He clings to the cold ground, as if to prevent Himself from being drawn farther from God. . . . The humanity of the Son of God trembled in that trying hour. He prayed not now for His disciples that their faith might not fail, but for His own tempted, agonized soul. The awful moment had come—that moment which was to decide the destiny of the world. The fate of humanity trembled in the balance." [5] Surely here, if God could have changed His mind concerning His working out of the plan of salvation, He would have.

However, the entire Bible, including the book of Jonah, consistently witnesses to an omniscient God, meaning He is all-wise. God does not need to learn. He doesn't mature. But that doesn't need to cause us any concern, because God already knows everything. He says so Himself: "I am God, and there is no one like me, declaring the end from the beginning and from ancient times things not yet done, saying, 'My purpose shall stand, and I will fulfill my intention'" (Isa. 46:9, 10, NRSV). "The former things I declared long ago, they went out from my mouth and I made them known; then suddenly I did them and they came to pass" (Isa. 48:3, NRSV).

God is all-powerful, omnipotent, and all-wise. The prophets—and God Himself—express this fact many times. All Scripture, including the book of Jonah, underscore the Lord's sovereign attributes. This is one reason His pursuing of Jonah is so impressive.

When Jonah fled from the presence of the Lord, that *might* have changed everything. As Jonah paid the fare to Tarshish, that *could* have been the end of God's plan and the prophet's relationship to Him. And when we have disobeyed, when we have tried to escape what God has convicted us about—when God has said one thing and you and I have done another—that *could* have been the end of us, too.

But this is *not* the end of the story of Jonah. God stays right with him. As Ellen White notes: "Not for long was he permitted to go on undisturbed in his mad flight."[6] As a result of Jonah's decision we find in his book one surprise after another as God pursues Jonah. The Lord did not take Jonah's negative response passively. However, He did not forsake him either. In the narrative we find God following him relentlessly, even using His arsenal of nature. For after the ship Jonah boarded has set sail "the Lord sent out a great wind on the sea" (Jonah 1:4).

As the narrative unfolds, we come upon a striking indicator of God's being. Here and throughout the four chapters of the book of Jonah the author dramatically reminds us that the God of heaven and earth is in control of His creation. It reflects the picture of God's sovereignty over His created world that we find through all Scripture. Both the Old Testament and the New Testament unfalteringly and continually ascribe the natural world as being under God's control. Jeremiah the prophet insists:

"Behold, the tempest of Yahweh: wrath has appeared, a whirling tempest which bursts over the heads of the wicked. Yahweh's anger will not turn back until He has accomplished and carried out the purpose of his mind" (Jer. 23:19, 20, paraphrase).

The psalmists also express the same sentiment:

"Praise Him, you heavens of heavens, and you waters above the heavens! . . . Praise the Lord from the earth . . . ; fire and hail, snow and clouds; stormy wind, fulfilling His word" (Ps. 148:4-8).

"Those who go down to the sea in ships, who do business on great waters, they see the works of the Lord, and His wonders in the deep. For he commands and raises the storm wind, which lifts up the waves of the seas. They mount up to the heavens, they go down again to the depths; their soul melts because of trouble. . . . He calms the storm, so that its waves are still" (Ps. 107:23-29).

The Lord of heaven and earth not only created but also rules the earth. The Bible writers insist that He forms the mountains (Amos 4:13) and removes them (Job 9:5; Amos 1:2; Micah 1:3, 4). At His presence they quake (Judges 5:5; Ps. 18:7; 68:8; 114:4-6; Isa. 64:3; Eze. 3:12; Hab. 3:6, 10).

In one of Amos's oracles we find God controlling the rain with the resulting famine used as a means of discipline:

"I gave you cleanness of teeth in all your cities, and lack of bread in all your places, yet you did not return to me, says the Lord. And I also withheld the rain from you when there were still three months to the harvest; I would send rain on one city, and send no rain on another city; one field would be rained upon, and the field on which it did not rain withered; so two or three towns wandered to one town to drink water, and were not satisfied; yet you did not return to me, says the Lord" (Amos 4:6-8, NRSV).

In the New Testament the apostle Paul also insists on the close relationship between God and His creation. "For the earnest expectation of the creation eagerly waits for the revealing of the sons of God. For the creation was subjected to futility, not willingly, but because of Him who subjected it in hope; because the creation itself also will be delivered from the bondage of corruption into the glorious liberty of the children of God. For we know that the whole creation groans and labors with birth pangs together until now" (Rom. 8:19-22).

Second Peter 3 reminds last-day scoffers about God's destruction of wickedness through the Flood. The disciple sees this earthwide destruction as undergirding the certainty of the world's final annihilation. Over against some contemporary thinking that views the universe as a closed system that allows no place for God's action within His creation, the Bible consistently confesses that all nature functions under divine control.

The ancient nation of Egypt learned this fundamental principle of God's sovereignty reluctantly through the increasing intensity of the 10 plagues that devastated their nation. Yes, God gives life's rich blessings to His creatures by means of the natural world. But He can also bring judgment through the same forces (Ex. 12:21-33).

"Ruin and desolation marked the path of the destroying angel," Ellen G. White writes of Egypt. "The land of Goshen alone was spared. It was demonstrated to the Egyptians that the earth is under the control of the living God, that the elements obey His voice, and that the only safety is in obedience to Him."[7]

As the Bible closes, the book of Revelation informs us that the whole world will find itself involved in a similar situation before the second coming of Christ:

"The time is at hand when there will be sorrow in the world that no human balm can heal. The Spirit of God is being withdrawn. Disasters by sea and by land follow one another in quick succession. How frequently we hear of earthquakes and tornadoes, of destruction by fire and flood, with great loss of life and property! Apparently these calamities are capricious outbreaks of disorganized, unregulated forces of nature, wholly beyond the control of man; but in them all, God's purpose may be read. They are among the agencies by which He seeks to arouse men and women to a sense of their danger."[8]

God has established laws in nature. But they do not administer themselves. The Lawgiver controls them. He has arranged a series of causes and effects and placed them in various relationships toward one another, sometimes in ways beyond our comprehension. According to Scripture, He supports, maintains, controls, and moves them at His own pleasure. We find this is a consistent refrain all through Scripture, no matter who is writing:

"He sends [note the verb in the present tense] the springs into the valleys; they flow among the hills. They give drink to every beast of the field; the wild donkeys quench their thirst. By them the birds of the heavens have their home; they sing among the branches. He waters the hills from His upper chambers; the earth is satisfied with the fruit of Your works" (Ps. 104:10-13).

"Your faithfulness endures to all generations; You established the earth, and it abides. They continue this day according to Your ordinances, for all are Your servants" (Ps. 119:90, 91).

"Praise Him, sun and moon; praise Him, all you stars of light! Praise Him, you heavens of heavens, and you waters above the heavens! Let them praise the name of the Lord, for He commanded, and they were created. He also established them forever and ever: *He made a decree which shall not pass away.* Praise the Lord from the earth, you great sea creatures and all the depths; fire and hail, snow and clouds; stormy wind, *fulfilling His word"* (Ps. 148:3-8).

"The Lord will open to you His good treasure, the heavens, to give the rain to your land in its season, and to bless all the work of your hand" (Deut. 28:12).

The apostle Paul bursts into doxology when he considers God's power: "For of Him and through Him and to Him are all things, to whom be glory forever. Amen" (Rom. 11:36).

Ellen White is consistent with the biblical witness when she speaks of God's providence: "It is by the mighty power of the Infinite One that the elements of nature in earth and sea and sky are kept within bounds. And these elements He uses for the happiness of His creatures."[9]

The Reformers were not ignorant of this important biblical perspective. For example, Martin Luther was sensitive to the miracles involved with God's present providence when he commented on one of Christ's miracles:

"The miracle of the cure of the deaf-and-dumb man is insignificant compared to what God does every day. For every day children are born who previously had neither ears nor tongues, nor indeed even a soul. In less than a year they are furnished with soul, body, tongue, and everything else. But this miracle is so common that no one pays any attention to it. Scarcely anyone in the world ever says thank you to God for his tongue and his ears. How many are there who having enjoyed good sight for fifty years ever give God thanks with all their hearts? How many rejoice over so great a miracle? They marvel that Christ healed this man, but not that they themselves are able to hear. By this little miracle God stirs us up to recognize the great miracles. The whole world is deaf not to hear this. Pythagoras was considered a heretic because he heard the wonderful song of the stars. But one who is not blind will see the heavens so wondrous that one could die for very joy over the sight."[10]

Thus it should not surprise us at all when the book of Jonah reveals God's sovereignty over nature: "The Lord sent out . . ." The biblical author recognizes God's hand at work as he attributes the storm not merely to the elements of nature, but to the God of nature.

God's hurling the stormy wind in the book of Jonah is no mere arbitrary display of divine power. He unleashes the tempest for Jonah's sake. Jonah 1:4 informs us that this storm is there for Jonah and because of Jonah. It causes the obviously normal effects of waves lashing the ocean, tossing ships about, panicking sailors. The storm endangers not only the many others on board Jonah's ship, but undoubtedly other ships on the sea at that time. As the narrative proceeds, we will find that this powerful storm threatens many who had no share in or even knowledge of Jonah's guilt. But its purpose is to confront the stubborn prophet. And by the end of the fourth chapter of the book of Jonah, we will more fully appreciate just how stubborn Jonah prophet is.

Right in the opening verses of the book of Jonah a "great wind" begins to blow. The reader finds a tempest brewing because God is stirring. We will find that this is only the beginning of the great lengths that God is willing to go to show how much He loves both the prophet and Nineveh. The storm indicates His special grace. The fact that God would go to such great pains with Jonah is not a sign of a vindictive attitude. According to Scripture, it demonstrates that He loves deeply. The book of Hebrews expresses this very point: "For whom the Lord loves He chastens, and scourges every son whom He receives" (Heb. 12:6). *Scourge* means "to whip with thongs." It is never a pleasant experience when it happens.

We can also begin to see in the first verses of the book of Jonah the seriousness of a God-given vocation. The Lord thinks His choice of messenger is so crucial and takes the person He elected so seriously that He brings nature into play to nudge Jonah to fulfill his task. And as God wrestled with Jacob at the brook Jabbok, so now He begins to struggle with Jonah, employing the very elements of nature in the process.

[1] E. G. White, *Patriarchs and Prophets,* p. 254.

[2] *Ibid.,* p. 255.

[3] J. R. Edwards, *The Divine Intruder,* p. 93.

[4] White, *Prophets and Kings,* p. 266.

[5] White, *The Desire of Ages,* pp. 686-690.

[6] White, *Prophets and Kings,* p. 267.

[7] *Ibid.,* p. 269.

[8] White, *Prophets and Kings,* p. 277.

[9] *Ibid.,* p. 134.

[10] Martin Luther, "The Cure of the Deaf and Dumb," in *The Book of Jesus: A Treasury of the Greatest Stories and Writings About Christ,* ed. Calvin Miller (New York: Simon and Schuster, 1998), p. 238.

A HEBREW PROPHET
AND A "HEATHEN" SKIPPER

The Mediterranean Sea churns under the fury of a major storm. It is so severe that the first chapter of the book of Jonah describes the sailors aboard Jonah's ship as so terrified that "every man cried out to his god" (Jonah 1:5). These experienced sailors realize that it is no ordinary storm and that it threatens grave danger. It is a critical moment. And they are constrained to pray. But where is Jonah?

As we noted earlier, Jonah 1:3 alludes twice to Jonah's downward course as he tries to flee "from the presence of the Lord." Just two verses later we see that the runaway prophet is still headed in the same direction as he goes "down into the lowest parts of the ship" and then lies "down." Jonah keeps *going down* and *down* and *down* in his miscalculated attempts to escape his divine commission. In the midst of a dangerous storm, when everyone else on board is struggling against the life-threatening elements, we find him doing nothing to help. Instead he retires to the bottom of the ship and sleeps.

One wonders how Jonah could sleep at a time like this. Can you imagine anyone sleeping in such a storm? Jesus once slept on board a ship during a dangerous storm on the Sea of Galilee. But Jonah's nap is hardly the sleep of faith. No, during the entire book of Jonah we will never find the prophet in such a positive attitude.

In the meantime, the storm on the Mediterranean rages. Ellen White describes how even the sea captain was "distressed beyond measure."[1] The biblical narrative pictures the concerned captain checking the ship from stem to stern. In the process he discovers someone sleeping. Astonished, he shouts to Jonah, "What do you mean, sleeper?" (verse 6a). And he begs Jonah, "Arise, call on your God" (verse 6b).

As we continue sensitizing our skills in reading biblical narratives, we notice here the striking similarity between the captain's command to Jonah to "arise" with God's initial mandate to Jonah to "arise." The captain's order must have startled Jonah. They are the very words *["qum lek"]* with which God had initially summoned the prophet. Moreover, the captain begs him to "cry" to God, again using the same verb that the Lord had when He told Jonah to "cry" against Nineveh (verse 2). Now, however, the summons to Jonah comes from a foreign sea captain who doesn't even know who Jonah's deity is. Nevertheless he pleads with him to intercede with his God.

The captain, even though an idolater, apparently realizes that mere humans cannot manipulate the gods. Notice how he implores Jonah: "call on your God; perhaps your God will consider us, so that we may not perish" (verse 6). We will recognize the same mature perception later among the pagan Ninevites in chapter 3. The captain, like his men, also senses that the storm is not a normal one. He is open to the possibility of some god being responsible. One can't help appreciating this enlightened pagan sea captain who seems to grasp what is going on. Especially striking is the irony of a non-Israelite skipper pleading with a Hebrew prophet to pray.

Apparently Jonah then prays as requested. Ellen White comments that "the prayers of the man who had turned aside from the path of duty brought no help."[2] However, it is the sailors who continue taking the initiative, convicted that the storm's overpowering violence is pointing to divine anger. In their desperation "they said to one another, 'Come, let us cast lots, that we may know for whose cause this trouble has come upon us.' So they cast lots, and the lot fell on Jonah" (verse 7).

By casting lots the mariners assume that a storm of such magnitude is somehow bound up with someone's misdeeds. Finding the culprit would help to determine whose guilt has triggered a deity to such extreme anger.

People in ancient times widely regarded casting lots as an appropriate method for decision-making. We find several examples in

Scripture, such as when the Israelites were going to divide their inheritance of the Promised Land (Num. 33:54). The accounts of Achan's thievery (Joshua 7) and of Saul's rash oath (1 Sam. 14:41, 42) depict the casting of lots to determine guilt, just as we find here in the book of Jonah. The book of Esther also records lot casting to seek divine guidance. We even find a commentary on the drawing of lots in Proverbs 16:33: "The lot is cast into the lap, but its every decision is from the Lord."

In the book of Jonah, as elsewhere in the Old Testament, we see God superintending the outcome. Attention now focuses on the reason for the storm. The casting of the lot reveals Jonah to be at fault. The sailors frantically beg him, "Tell us, now! On whose account has this calamity struck us?" (Jonah 1:8, NASB). According to ancient custom, the outcome of lot casting needed the corroboration of the convicted person before justice could be administered. This gave Jonah the opportunity to deny or confirm the accusation.

The sailors quickly raise a series of questions: "What is your occupation? And where do you come from? What is your country? And of what people are you?" (verse 8) The men are desperately attempting to identify the god that Jonah has offended. Thus they seek to learn where he is from, and the people to which he belongs. All or any of this information might help them solve the deadly emergency.

Up to this point in the narrative Jonah has said nothing at all. Now, in response to all the questions put to him, he answers only two of them. "So he said to them, 'I am a Hebrew; and I fear the Lord, the God of heaven, who made the sea and the dry land'" (verse 9). Jonah understands the intent of the questions. Notice how he especially evades the one that would reveal his occupation as a prophet. Since other Near Easterners, such as the Philistines and the Egyptians, knew the Israelites as Hebrews (Gen. 39:14; Ex. 1:15; 1 Sam. 14:21, 22), it is not surprising to find Jonah admitting that he is a Hebrew. He also confesses that he fears "the Lord, the God of heaven," the one supreme and true God. The name "the God of heaven" is how Daniel, another prophet, calls upon the Lord when he pleads for understanding of Nebuchadnezzar's dream (Dan. 2:19).

In his confession Jonah also uses another name of God: "the Lord"

(Yahweh), very familiar in the Old Testament, starting with the Creation account in Genesis.[3] In fact, it is the unique, personal covenant name for the God of the Bible. Jonah thus declares that the God he worships is not merely a nationalistic tribal deity—He is the Lord, the true God of heaven.

Jonah glibly makes his dramatic declaration that he "fears" Yahweh at a time when he is in full flight from God and a rebel against His will. He thinks that he can ignore God's bidding and yet count himself a true believer. We find Jonah paying lip service to His God even though he is the cause behind a vicious storm that could possibly drown an entire shipful of people.

Jonah further identifies his God as the one "who made the sea and the dry land" (Jonah 1:9b). We find this phrase used for the Creator elsewhere in the Old Testament (Gen. 1:10; Ps. 95:5). No doubt Jonah is oblivious to the fact that he is actually confirming himself as the cause of the storm by his confession of faith in the One who has the sea under His control!

An additional element of irony now surfaces. Jonah did not want to carry the Word of God to Nineveh. But now, in his mad flight from that assignment, he finds himself forced to testify of his God to the pagan sailors on the ship.

As we read this narrative, it might become very easy to be critical of someone such as Jonah. It is much harder to recognize the same attitude in ourselves. Jonah's confession should remind us of what we sometimes do. Have we declared our allegiance to the God of heaven and His remnant church while covering up that we too are "fleeing" from some direct instruction God gave us? Do we ever speak of our faith in God and at the same time refuse His counsel to us?

The biblical account records the sailors' immediate reaction to Jonah's response to their questions: "Then the men became extremely frightened" (Jonah 1:10, NASB). The prophet's declaration of his God caused the sailors to be "exceedingly afraid." They were already afraid of the storm (verse 5). The text now discloses that they *greatly* fear the God of heaven. Thus they react more apprehensively to Jonah's confession about God than they did to the perilous storm.

The narrative continues its subtle painting of the striking contrast between the pagan sailors and Jonah. While Jonah, a prophet of God, dares to act contrary to his God, the mere mention of the mighty God of heaven triggers great alarm in the hearts of the sailors. They are convinced that it is foolish to tangle with such a powerful deity. However, their conviction didn't arise because Jonah courageously testified for his God. No, he made his confession only because of their questions. But despite that, his disclosure stirred the mariners' hearts.

Another issue needs addressing at this point. We find no evidence in the conversation between Jonah and the sailors of the religious "pluralism" or "ecumenism" so often urged today—that all the different religions are all really worshiping the same divine being. Both Jonah and the sailors knew very well that they weren't all somehow worshiping the same God! Rather, as the frightened mariners continue their interrogation, they urge Jonah: "Why have you done this?" (verse 10). The terrified sailors now express horror at Jonah's flight from the God of heaven and earth. The Hebrew language reveals at this point that the sailors' fear again increases.

Although the sailors are asking an urgent question, the words also express astonishment that anyone would have the audacity to take such liberties with such a God. They dread the thought of what may happen, for they stand in awe of this great God, knowing that they are at His mercy as they struggle against the elements. The mighty storm powerfully preached the omnipotence of the God of heaven. It impressed the sailors despite Jonah's terrible behavior. They certainly saw nothing particularly impressive in him. In fact, what moved them was that they saw he had disobeyed the God of heaven and earth. But through all this, they recognized that there is a real God, a deity who was in control! The Lord broke through to the sailors in an amazing way in spite of His recalcitrant prophet.

At this juncture in the narrative we find repeated for the third time in the space of just a few verses the phrase "from the presence of the Lord." It has occurred in this first chapter almost like a refrain. As you recall, we have already seen it twice in verse 3. The author of the book of Jonah, as with all biblical writers, is deliberate in his choice of words. Biblical narrative writers employed repetition of words or phrases as a technique to alert the reader to significant points they wanted to emphasize. In this case the author has deliberately focused the reader's attention on Jonah's obstinate attitude as he attempts to evade his responsibility.

The sailors grow more desperate as the storm worsens. They realize that something must be done or everyone will perish. And, continuing to take the initiative, they appeal to Jonah: "What shall we do to you?" (verse 11). Earlier they had acknowledged the God that Jonah worshiped. Now they ask the prophet what they should do. The sailors admit their fear and beg his cooperation: "What can we do so that God will not be angry? Please tell us and we will obey." Having established that Jonah, on his own admission after the casting of lots, is evading his God-given task, the crew finally turns to him as the one at fault. Surely he should know what to do in such desperate circumstances.

The culprit now has no choice but to admit that his guilt should be punished. The situation should have evoked from Jonah an immediate confession of wrongdoing coupled with a prayer for forgiveness. He then should have petitioned God to deliver everyone from death at sea. But even now Jonah refuses to admit that he is wrong.

The contrast between the pagan sailors and Jonah in the first chapter of the book of Jonah is remarkable. The mariners display a level of morality that should shame him. He hasn't been willing to accept the fact that the pagan Ninevites are worthy of receiving a message from God. Yet pagan sailors express respect for the Hebrew prophet's life and his God while all through this storm Jonah dares to act contrary to the will of the God whom he claims to serve. Accordingly, at this point, Jonah urges the sailors to "pick me up and throw me into the sea; then the sea will become calm for you. For I know that this great tempest is because of me" (verse 12).

At first glance Jonah's solution may appear courageous and altruistic. However, it actually masks continuing disobedience. If neither his flight nor his nap has saved Jonah from the divine imperatives, then at least drowning will. Don't be mistaken—Jonah is no pious martyr. The prophet realizes that he deserves death for his obstinate disobedience. He knows what the Hebrew Scriptures teach about wickedness. In fact, he even admits that he has put everyone on board ship in jeopardy. But he stubbornly wants to drown rather than admit his wrongdoing or fulfill his divine mission.

Jonah never shows any remorse for the danger in which he has placed everyone. He makes no confession to God or anyone else. Having decided to disobey God, he is prepared to drown in the raging sea rather than change his mind. Perhaps he surmises that once he is dead the storm will abate because it will have fulfilled its purpose. It could be that Jonah decides that his just punishment will then allow the ship to continue on its way safely.

What might have happened if Jonah had repented of his defection right then and there and pleaded for God to save him, the crew, and the ship? Later the apostle Paul also experienced a terrible storm on board a ship in the same body of water. However, during that storm Paul took command of the situation and exhibited an attitude quite different from Jonah's. Courageously he declared:

"Take courage! . . . Last night an angel of the God to whom I belong and whom I serve stood beside me, and he said, 'Don't be afraid, Paul, for you will surely stand trial before Caesar! What's more, God in His goodness has granted safety to everyone sailing with you.' So take courage! For I believe God. It will be just as he said" (Acts 27:21-25, NLT).

Ellen White writes concerning Paul's storm at sea:

"I saw that God's special purpose was fulfilled in the journey of Paul upon the sea; He designed that the ship's crew might thus witness the power of God through Paul and that the heathen also might hear the name of Jesus, and that many might be converted through the teaching of Paul and by witnessing the miracles he wrought."[4]

Jonah lost a wonderful opportunity to witness positively to the God of heaven and earth.

The narrative in Jonah 1 continues to paint the contrast between a Hebrew prophet and "heathen" non-Israelite mariners. Jonah had not thought the Assyrians worthy of repentance. Yet on their ship to Tarshish Gentile sailors persist in displaying a higher sense of morality than the Hebrew prophet himself. They show themselves willing to do everything in their power to save Jonah's skin even though the sea is becoming "more and more violent against them" (Jonah 1:13b,

Amplified). However, the increasing intensity of an already dangerous storm finally forces them to make a difficult decision, but only after they have first struggled even more desperately in an effort to reach the shore. But they cannot, for the sea continues to "grow more tempestuous against them" (verse 13).

Notice how Jonah's solution appears too drastic to the sailors. They continue to exhibit respect for the man's life even though his disobedience has put all their lives in danger. Somehow, they desperately hope, perhaps they might still make it safely to land and save his life. Jonah has pronounced sentence against himself, but the sailors do not at once lay hands upon him. Instead they strive even harder to get back to land and avoid the risk of bloodshed. Frantically they continue struggling to reach shore. At this critical moment, again it is the sailors—not Jonah—who pray to Yahweh. "Therefore they cried out to the Lord and said, 'We pray, O Lord, please do not let us perish for this man's life, and do not charge us with innocent blood; for You, O Lord, have done as it pleased You" (verse 14).

Let us pause briefly and ponder this amazing prayer of confession and contrition to the Lord, God of heaven. Here, supposedly pagan Gentiles, face to face with a rebellious Israelite prophet, fear to put him to death. And they pray to his God that they won't be guilty of Jonah's death. This is one of the most amazing prayers in all Scripture. It is not the Hebrew prophet praying for the pagan sailors, but the other way around!

Their second petition to God—"Do not charge us with innocent blood"—implies that the mariners hold to an ethical standard that prohibits murder. They call upon Jonah's God to witness that they are not criminals. And they plead that He will not hold them guilty of the prophet's death. Their petition—"Please do not let us perish for this man's life"—also implies their conviction that the God of heaven judges human actions and that He can be appealed to for justice. Again we find pronounced irony: non-Israelites, face to face with a disobedient Hebrew prophet, pray that they will not acquire guilt through his death.

The sailors use God's special covenant name Yahweh, or Lord, for apparently they have accepted Jonah's testimony in verse 9. Their prayer also suggests a faith that God will hear and answer their request. The incident presents us with amazing evidence for an inclination toward the true God in the pagan world. Only Jonah, God's prophet, remains silent at this point, even in the face of death. At last, however, the violence of the storm finally constrains the sailors to pick up Jonah and throw, or hurl, him into the sea (verse 15a).

Here we encounter the book's fourth use of the verb "to hurl," which, along with several other key words and phrases, echoes throughout this chapter. The Hebrew root "to hurl" is not common in the Old Testament. However, it occurs four times in this chapter, as if to underscore the strength of God's actions and their results. In this case it draws attention to the violent act made necessary by Jonah's stubborn will.

Our close reading of the text again instructs us that this type of word repetition is not a result of the writer's limited vocabulary. Recurring words and phrases, so prominent in Hebrew narrative writing, serve as the narrator's way of marking something for emphasis. They can also point to larger enveloping or mirroring structures that repeat initial themes at the conclusion of a section. We find this particular phenomenon right at the opening and closing of chapter 1. When the sailors throw Jonah overboard, "the sea stopped its raging" (verse 15, NASB), which completes the action initiated in verse 4, in which "a great storm" (NASB) arose. Again we encounter evidence that we are reading skillfully composed Hebrew narrative writing.

At the precise instant that Jonah plunges into the raging waters, "the sea stopped its raging" (verse 15b, NASB). Once again we find the sovereign God of heaven and earth in full control of nature. As we discussed earlier, it is a frequent occurrence in Scripture. Christ demonstrated the same power over His creation in the New Testament when He stilled the storm on the Sea of Galilee: "Then He arose and rebuked the wind, and said to the sea, 'Peace, be still!' And the wind ceased and there was a great calm" (Mark 4:39).

Returning to the book of Jonah, we must notice the perceptive reaction of the pagan sailors to the sudden change in the weather: "And the sea ceased from her raging. Then the men feared the Lord exceedingly, and offered a sacrifice unto the Lord, and made vows"

(Jonah 1:15b, 16, KJV). The immediate calming of the storm so strikingly manifested the omnipotent arm of the holy God of heaven and earth that now the sailors "feared the Lord [Yahweh] with great fear" (verse 16, paraphrase). Jonah 1:4, 5 describes how they had *feared* the storm, but at this instant they fear the *God* of the storm *exceedingly*, their response now intensified to the superlative degree. Sturdy sailors who earlier had prayed to an array of false gods now worship Yahweh and make vows to Him. Their lives are dramatically altered because they have come into contact with the living God. They make such offerings as they can then and there. But they do even more, commiting themselves to vows that they will carry out later.

Their offering sacrifices is highly significant. They see the need of atonement outside themselves. Even the order is significant. The sailors make their vows after the sacrifice, after the blood atonement. They don't make vows in order to precipitate God's mercy. Rather, they behold His power in the storm and in Jonah's reluctant confession and then become converted to the true God and make sacrifices to Him. Jonah didn't want to bring opportunity for salvation to the Ninevites. But now in the ship, quite outside of his plan, his life mediates salvation to the pagan sailors.

The verb "to fear" is another of the key words used in the book of Jonah. Jonah employs it in his discussion with the sailors—"I fear the Lord, the God of heaven" (verse 9). But his actions don't correspond with his confession, and are in direct contrast to the non-Israelite crew. The last we hear of them, we find that "the men feared the Lord greatly" (verse 16, KJV). And, unlike Jonah, their deeds parallel their convictions. Jonah mouths the words of a believer, but his behavior doesn't correspond. The sailors, by contrast, are genuinely in awe of Jonah's God. The writer's skillful contrast of Jonah with the pagan mariners confronts the alert reader with an example of a believer expressing faith in God while their heart is not converted. James Edwards is right when he declares:

"The contrasts between Jonah and the pagan sailors are sharp as broken glass . . . [and forces] us to reconsider our fast and pompous distinctions between righteous and wicked, saved and damned, elect and reprobate. No Gospel writer questioned those same distinctions more than St. Mark. In the first verse of his Gospel, Mark declares that Jesus Christ is the Son of God. But not until the crucifixion does it finally dawn on anyone in the story itself who Jesus really is. And who is that someone? Not a disciple, not even Peter. Like Jonah, the disciples have fled, along with the relatives and associates of Jesus. Not a Pharisee or member of the Sanhedrin, either. The first human being in the Gospel of Mark to recognize Jesus as the Son of God is not even a Jew, but a Roman, a 'Gentile sinner' as they were called. In fact, he was the captain of the squad of soldiers that executed Jesus! 'Surely this man was the Son of God!' said the centurion (Mark 15:39). What an irony for the followers of Jesus to find that a total outsider—indeed an enemy—was the first person to see into the heart of the [Christian] faith!"[5]

We have seen some strange twists thus far in the first chapter of the book of Jonah:

1. The prophet Jonah, although orthodox in his beliefs, responds to God in disobedience. He claims to fear God, but his actions contradict his confession. This contrasts directly with the mariners, who, though pagans, respond submissively to God's power as revealed through the casting of lots and the "great" storm.

2. Jonah would not go to Nineveh to preach to the Gentiles there, but he winds up in a situation in which his attempted escape from his divine directive brings pagans to believe in God. Through his defection a ship's crew acknowledges the Creator's power and comes to worship Him and acknowledge Him as Lord.

And we have only begun delving into this impressive narrative.

---

[1] E. G. White, *Prophets and Kings,* p. 267.

[2] *Ibid.*

[3] Also in Genesis 24:7; Ezra 5:11, 12; and when Daniel intercedes for his people (Dan. 9:4).

[4] White, *Early Writings* (Washington, D.C.: Review and Herald Pub. Assn., 1882, 1945), p. 207.

[5] J. R. Edwards, *The Divine Intruder,* pp. 96, 97.

Seven

SALVATION IS OF THE LORD!

*J*onah has been flung overboard into the Mediterranean. For all that the sailors know, he has drowned in the sea. However, at this very moment, God's control over the natural world again confronts the reader. Chapter 1 has already convincingly revealed this: God causing the great wind of a storm (verse 4); His controlling the casting of lots (verse 7); and His stopping the raging of the storm (verse 15).

And now at this very instant God further exhibits His sovereign power over creation for the fourth time in just this one chapter: "And the Lord appointed a great fish to swallow Jonah" (verse 17, NASB). Scripture regularly depicts the God of heaven and earth as directly involved in the carrying out of His purposes. In fact, this is His consistent assurance all through Scripture. No one can presume to limit His activity. Humans often try—even Jonah the prophet has said no to Him. But, the wind, the storm, and the fish obey.

In the original language the verb describing God's enlistment of the huge marine animal is unambiguous. The Old Testament elsewhere uses the verb "appointed" for "appointing" good gifts, such as God does with His steadfast love and faithfulness (Ps. 61:7), or in Babylon when the king "appointed" the diet for the select prisoners (Dan. 1:10). Now in Jonah 1:17 with Yahweh as the subject, the verb stresses God's sovereignty as He delegates a great fish to swallow Jonah.

This word "to appoint" does not mean to create. Rather, it involves God "ordaining" a great fish to swallow the prophet. He delegates or "commissions" a certain sea creature to accomplish a unique task. And by God's "appointment" the "great fish" is in exactly the right place at just the right time in order to ingest Jonah and confine

83

him safely within the deep waters of the Mediterranean.

The narrator will later couple this same verb with God three more times in the book of Jonah, thus constantly accentuating God's omnipotence. As we will find later in the fourth chapter, the Lord God will "appoint" a plant, a worm, and a scorching east wind. In each instance the text plainly indicates that God is ever sovereign over all His creation.

The author does not name the kind of fish, and whales are rare in the Mediterranean. However, readers should not get distracted by looking for such unimportant details as species names. Rather the writer wants us to focus on the miracle of the obedient creature, and the further miracle of Jonah being kept alive inside the "great fish."

The Hebrew verb "swallow" (Jonah 1:17), describing the great fish's action, includes the nuance of "engulfing." The book of Jonah couples it with a specific prefix expressing purpose. Other Old Testament usages link the verb with God's judging activity: "The Lord will swallow them up in His wrath, and fire will devour them" (Ps. 21:9, NASB). The prophet Jeremiah uses the imagery to describe the king of Babylon's military activity. "Nebuchadezzer the king of Babylon has devoured me, he has crushed me; he has made me an empty vessel, he has swallowed me up like a monster; he has filled his stomach with my delicacies, he has spit me out" (Jer. 51:34).

As he flounders in the Mediterranean, Jonah assumes that he is drowning. But instead he finds himself sucked into a great dark and smelly void. Jonah must have felt that he had reached the end of his life. However, against all odds, he finds himself alive!

In fact, this split-second timing of such a miraculous deliverance from a drowning death is still another striking evidence of divine providence operating in his life. Such unexpected "salvation" tells us more about God than it does of Jonah, however! Despite his profound disobedience, Jonah experiences the power of God preserving him from death. And the miracles aren't over yet. The prophet survives "three days and three nights" (Jonah 1:17) in a most unusual type of aquatic transport.

Deep in the depths of the Mediterranean Jonah could hardly have known at first what caused the sudden dramatic change from drowning in a choking darkness to an even greater absolute blackness. It would have taken time for him to realize that the surrounding dark-ness was not that of Sheol, but that of an utterly unexpected safety. And when Jonah grasped that he was actually preserved alive, he re-garded it as a token of divine protection. At last he turns to God, and we finally hear him praying: "Then Jonah prayed to the Lord his God from the stomach of the fish" (Jonah 2:1, NASB).

His prayer puts into words the anguish he felt as he was drown-ing—his reaction on the brink of death, along with his experience and reflections within the "great fish." He borrows many phrases from the book of Psalms. And we become aware of just how well Jonah knew his Bible!

Using phrases from the book of Psalms as one prays is not an un-usual thing to do. Because of their expressive quality, even today many Christians often frame at least part of their prayers with phrases from the Psalter. People also employ psalms in public worship invo-cations and benedictions.

Let us take a brief look at Jonah's prayer. Earlier on board ship during the storm the sea captain had begged Jonah to pray (Jonah 1:16). The pagan crew of the ship had been moved to pray (verse 14), taking the initiative that we might have expected a Hebrew prophet to assume. At last, here in his extremity, Jonah earnestly prays. And the opening words of his prayer echo prayers in the Psalms, such as:

> "In my distress I called upon the Lord,
> And cried out to my God;
> He heard my voice from His temple,
> And my cry came before Him, even to His ears" (Ps. 18:6).

Finally Jonah finds himself driven to implore God even when it might seem too late for prayer. He has stubbornly tried to evade God, and even inside the fish he is still close to death. In fact, the next phrase of his prayer expresses his extreme anguish as he thinks he is drowning: "I cried for help from the depth [or "belly"] of Sheol; You heard my voice" (Jonah 2:2, NASB).

Jonah's expression "from . . . Sheol" in the original language im-plies a hopeless situation, indicating that he realizes the extreme na-ture of his circumstances as he hangs in the very jaws of death itself. And he acknowledges God's control of this situation:

"For You had cast me into the deep,
Into the heart of the seas,
And the current engulfed me.
All Your breakers and billows passed over me" (verse 3, NASB).

The prophet surely was aware that it was the ship's crew who had thrown him overboard (Jonah 1:15). Yet he now admits that it was the Lord Himself who had been at work, and that the sailors had but unwittingly been only fulfilling the Lord's purpose. Since he knew his Bible, Jonah was aware of how the Lord often uses human agents in furthering His purposes. For example, God declares through the prophet Isaiah: "Woe to Assyria, the rod of My anger, and the staff in whose hand is My indignation" (Isa. 10:5).

The word "current" (nahar) in Jonah 2:3, which Jonah mentions engulfing him, recalls Psalm 93:3, 4. The word appears here in the book of Jonah in its plural form (neharot—floods) with a three-time repetition underscoring the power of the storm. However, the psalmist insists on the even greater power of the Lord on high:

"The floods have lifted up, O Lord,
The floods have lifted up their voice,
The floods lift up their pounding waves.
More than the sounds of many waters,
Than the mighty breakers of the sea,
The Lord on high is mighty" (Ps. 93:3, 4, NASB).

Jonah also acknowledges that the breaking sea that swept over him was under the Lord's control, employing words that echo the psalmist who prayed: "All Your breakers and Your waves have rolled over me" (Ps 42:7b, NASB). Jonah too has felt similar anguish: "For You cast me into the deep, into the heart of the seas, and the floods surrounded me; all Your billows and Your waves passed over me" (Jonah 2:3).

At this point Jonah's feeling of desperation is clear. The use of the personal pronoun in the original language is emphatic and underscores Jonah's anxiety. "Then I said, 'I am driven away from your sight!'" (verse 4a, NRSV). It would have been more honest, however, for Jonah to admit that he had fled "from the presence of the Lord," as the author reminds us three times in chapter 1!

Continuing our close reading of the text, we recall that the verb "driven" that Jonah uses here also appears in Genesis 3:24, recording Adam and Eve's banishment from the Garden of Eden: "So He [God] drove the man out [of the garden of Eden]" (NASB). Jonah understood that he was experiencing God's profound punishment as he was drowning. Yet he perceives that in spite of everything he has done God has actually spared his life.

The next phrase in his prayer is striking: "Yet I will look again toward Your holy temple" (Jonah 2:4b). Many have seen this exclamation as the center of his prayer. Jonah finally finds himself constrained to admit God's mercy, long after the pagan sailors have done so. But the watery ordeal is not yet over. Jonah continues by describing his initial helpless descent through the depths of the sea:

"Water encompassed me to the point of death.
The great deep engulfed me,
Weeds were wrapped around my head.
I descended to the roots of the mountains.
The earth with its bars was around me forever"
    (verses 5, 6a, NASB).

The prophet here relives the process of drowning. The four-line description expresses his despair of ever escaping death's clutches and marks the extremity of his plunge into the Mediterranean.

When the text records that the prophet was "in the belly of the fish three days and three nights" (Jonah 1:17), it reminds us how agonizingly slow time seems to pass when one is suffering. Jonah describes his situation: "'The earth with its bars was around me forever'" (Jonah 2:6, NASB). The "bars" Jonah mentions as being around him perhaps allude to the rib cage of the "great fish."

The mention of "three days and three nights" should trigger our thinking to other textual usages of this formula of time passage. The phrase appears elsewhere in the Old Testament. In Genesis on the "third day" Abraham and Isaac received the indication from God that they had reached the mountain of sacrifice, from which Isaac would be miraculously delivered (Gen. 22:4). It also occurs in another life-and-death context in which David found the Egyptian slave who had been left to die and had not eaten for "three days and three nights"

(1 Sam. 30:12). Later, King Hezekiah, when critically ill, received the promise that "on the third day" he would go up to the house of the Lord (2 Kings 20:5, 8).

The New Testament also employs this particular time marker. Jesus refers to "the sign of the prophet Jonah," using the same time period of "three days and three nights" for His own burial and resurrection (Matt. 12:39, 40; see also Luke 11:30). He thus relates Jonah's miraculous deliverance from death to His own passion.

In his prayer from the "great fish" Jonah speaks of "Sheol" and of "the pit," terms the Old Testament uses to describe death. The prophet Hosea, speaking within the general time frame when Jonah's experience would likely still have been referred to, utilizes Jonah's chronological formula within a resurrection motif: "After two days He will revive us; on the third day He will raise us up" (Hosea 6:2):

"Hosea 6:1-3 clearly refers to Israel's captivity and restoration as a 'death' and 'resurrection' on the 'third day,' parallel to the experience of Jonah. From this allusion it appears that Hosea envisions Israel as recapitulating the experience of Jonah in their 'death-resurrection' experience." [1]

Thus, when Christ compares His death and resurrection experience to that of Jonah, He is linking it with the Old Testament understanding.

Jonah's prayer allows us to hear what he believed were his last thoughts as a dying man. However, the runaway prophet's worst fears are not realized. He doesn't drown. Though he is now in a unfathomable darkness, God has indeed not taken his life. And as a result, there comes a reversal of his despair:

> "But You have brought up my life from the pit, O Lord my God.
> While I was fainting away,
> I remembered the Lord,
> And my prayer came to You,
> Into Your holy temple" (verses 6c, 7, NASB).

Jonah's use of the phrase "Your holy temple" employs the language used by other prophets for the heavenly sanctuary, such as: "The Lord is in his holy temple; the Lord's throne is in heaven. His eyes behold, his gaze examines humankind" (Ps. 11:4, NRSV). The prophet Micah also declares: "Hear, you peoples, all of you; listen, O earth and all it contains, and let the Lord God be a witness against you, the Lord from His holy temple" (Micah 1:2, NASB). The prophet Habakkuk speaks similarly: "But the Lord is in His holy temple. Let all the earth keep silence before Him" (Hab. 2:20).

Though disobedient, Jonah realizes that his remoteness in the depths of the sea has not blocked his prayer. By faith, he trusts God in His heavenly sanctuary! However, God does not immediately deliver the prophet from his watery "cavern." Jonah's prayer does not suggest that he is out of the great fish on dry land. Rather it emphasizes that his location in the depths of the sea has proven no barrier to God's hearing his prayer. Jonah believes that the Lord has not ultimately forsaken him. He has already experienced, through his miraculous "salvation" in the sea, that God's power is as vast as His knowledge of those who call on Him for help. Jonah experiences the reality of the great psalm of God's omniscience:

"Where can I go from your spirit?
Or where can I flee from your presence?
If I ascend to heaven, you are there;
if I make my bed in Sheol, you are there.
If I take the wings of the morning
and *settle at the farthest limits of the sea,*
even there your hand shall lead me,
and your right hand shall hold me fast.
If I say, 'Surely the darkness shall cover me,
and the light around me become night,'
even the darkness is not dark to you;
the night is as bright as the day,
for darkness is as light to you" (Ps. 139:7-12, NRSV).

Jonah now expresses the futility of trusting false deities:

"Those who regard vain idols
Forsake their faithfulness" (Jonah 2:8, NASB).

The terms applied to the idols include the sense of insubstantial, purposeless, emptiness and worthlessness. False gods are deceptive because they are not what they claim to be. In fact, they have no existence at all. Jonah is convinced of the folly of forsaking the God of heaven and earth. And his prayer, which began with a desperate distress call to the Lord, concludes in a declaration of God's mercy:

"But I will sacrifice to You
With the voice of thanksgiving.
That which I have vowed I will pay.
Salvation is from the Lord" (verse 9, NASB).

Many have seen this final phrase of Jonah's prayer as the very center of the book of Jonah, the central point the writer wishes to emphasize. Again the personal pronoun is emphatic in the Hebrew language, adding intensity to the proclamation. James Edwards insightfully summarizes Jonah's amazing journey thus far: "Like a whale hit with a harpoon, the believer begins to fight. Excuses, protests, laments, pleas—all erupt from the volcano of the fully awakened soul, a soul that, if only for an instant, has perceived the awesome distance between God and itself. In contrast to the stormy human partner, God holds the rudder to a steady course, neither assailing in wrath nor recoiling in offense, repeating the command again and again until the wearied soul collapses into the arms of a holy love that it has long sought but feared to trust."[2]

Jonah finally finds himself compelled to admit God's saving mercy, but, ironically, as we have already noted, long after the non-Israelite sailors have already done so. The Hebrew prophet Jonah's promise to sacrifice and make vows also belatedly follows the ship's pagan crew's (Jonah 1:16). Both chapters 1 and 2 end with the theme of sacrifice and vows, leading the reader to draw a parallel between prophet Jonah's experience and that of the pagan mariners. Both Jonah and the mariners:

❖ face an extreme crisis and peril from the storm;
❖ cry to Yahweh, acknowledging His sovereignty;
❖ are physically saved;
❖ offer worship.

Only, the mariners' faith long precedes that of the prophet Jonah! He at last comes to the same attitude that the Gentile ship crew had already reached.

The linking of sacrifice and vows is not unusual in the Old Testament. The psalmist prays:

"I will go into Your house with burnt offerings;
I will pay You my vows,
Which my lips have uttered
And my mouth has spoken when I was in trouble.
I will offer You burnt sacrifices of fat animals,
With the sweet aroma of rams;
I will offer bulls with goats" (Ps. 66:13-15).

The last words in Jonah's prayer—"Salvation is from the Lord" (Jonah 2:9b, NASB)—puts the emphasis where it belongs: on Yahweh, who has saved him. The word *yeshua* may be used of physical deliverance. But when it is applied to the work of God, it implies God's far-reaching purpose to save in the fullest sense. Many times the psalmist and the prophet wax eloquently of God as Savior:

"For God alone my soul waits in silence; from him comes my salvation. He alone is my rock and my salvation, my fortress; I shall never be shaken" (Ps. 62:1, 2, NRSV).

"It will be said on that day, Lo, this is our God; we have waited for him, so that he might save us. This is the Lord for whom we have waited; let us be glad and rejoice in his salvation" (Isa. 25:9, NRSV).

"The Lord has bared his holy arm before the eyes of all the nations; and all the ends of the earth shall see the salvation of our God" (Isa. 52:10, NRSV).

Jonah discovers divine grace when his situation is hopeless, when to all appearances he should expect nothing from God. The storm at sea has convinced Jonah that he cannot escape the Lord. He finally realizes that his rebellion is not a hidden matter, and that God is fully aware of his stubbornness. The biblical picture of God's grace to Jonah should greatly encourage us that God doesn't respond just to our better attitudes and feelings, but also to our desperate cries resulting from our disobedience!

This is an important point. In his entire prayer Jonah never confesses his rebelliousness. We see no indication that he is truly penitent. He never admits that he has been wrong, such as David cried to God in his repentance for his adultery:

"For I acknowledge my transgressions,
And my sin is ever before me.

91

> Against you, you alone, have I sinned,
> And done what is evil in your sight. . . .
> Create in me a clean heart, O God. . . .
> The sacrifice acceptable to God is a broken spirit;
> a broken and contrite heart, O God, you will not despise"
> (Ps. 51:3-17, NRSV).

And yet Jonah's prayer should reassure us that we can pray in the midst of failure, even when our own rebellion has created our distress. Even when we don't recognize our own guilt or feel sorry. This is a critical issue, because these are the very times it seems the most difficult to pray. It is often at such a time we feel that we have no right to call on God. Or even if we might want to pray, we feel that we surely don't deserve His help.

Jonah's experience should also be a great source of encouragement for us that God will not let us continue forever in our own personal rebellion against Him. Nothing could be worse than if He did not care enough for us to pursue us when we run away from Him. Thus we can take courage from Jonah's experience and thank God when He confronts us with our disobedience.

Notice how Jonah expresses his prayer in poetry. Some have suggested this fact as a reason that the story of Jonah can't be a true historical account. However, much of the Old Testament consists of poetry. For example, in the Creation narrative Adam bursts into poetry when he sees Eve for the first time (Gen. 2:23). The book of Genesis ends with Jacob blessing his sons. All 12 oracles take poetic form (Gen. 48:15–49:27). The historical book of Samuel opens with the exultant poetic prayer of Hannah (1 Sam. 2:1-10).

Even the numerous prophecies of the Old Testament are expressed in poetry. For example, the 66 chapters of the book of Isaiah include historical narrative. But when Isaiah speaks the words of God, he presents them in poetry. Chapter 6 contains both narrative describing Isaiah's prophetic call and the poetic conversation between the prophet and the seraph. Next, chapter 7 includes the narrative account of God's sending Isaiah to King Ahaz with a poetic prophetic message of courage in the face of a major Assyrian threat. The remainder of the book of Isaiah comprises mainly prophecies, the vast proportion couched in poetry.

In the past many English versions of the Bible were not formatted so that this characteristic linking of narrative and poetry was visually obvious. Fortunately, the more recent English translations have corrected this. Since up to 40 percent of the Old Testament is poetry, this is helpful to the reader.

The inclusion of poetry within narrative materials is not a valid reason to relegate the Old Testament to fiction and myth, as some modern scholars do. Nonbiblical ancient writings often used poetry within historical records. Presenting human history or prayers in poetry does not automatically categorize the material as an ancient myth. Bible writers may well have been sensitive to how poetic expression gives words their most profound and intense meaning. Thus to find Jonah praying in lyrical language would not have been unusual in Old Testament times.

But what happens to Jonah next? The surprises are not over!

---

[1] Richard M. Davidson, "New Testament Use of the Old Testament," *Journal of the Adventist Theological Society* 5, no. 1 (spring 1994): 30. Davidson continues: "It may also be more than coincidental that in the next chapter Hosea says Israel is 'like Jonah' . . . who flees from Yahweh . . . (Hosea 7:11, 13)."

[2] J. R. Edwards, *The Divine Intruder,* p. 92.

Eight

GOD OF
THE SECOND TIME

After Jonah prays, we catch another glimpse of the absolute sovereign power of God: "Then the Lord commanded the fish, and it vomited Jonah up onto the dry land" (Jonah 2:10, NASB). The text explicitly informs us that the "great fish" is not just nauseous from indigestion. Rather, the huge marine creature, already seen to be under divine direction (Jonah 1:17), is again impelled by God and obeys. The fish deposits Jonah on the beach.

What happens to him there? "Now the word of the Lord came to Jonah the second time" (Jonah 3:1). The prophet is right back where he started from. The first words of chapter 3 repeat the opening words of the book of Jonah. After a period of determined insubordination the prophet Jonah receives a second chance to obey. Surely these are some of the most heartwarming words in Scripture!

As we have seen, Jonah has deliberately and stubbornly rebelled against God. The marvel is that it does not make the Lord turn His back on the runaway prophet. He does not dismiss His servant because of his petulant disobedience. It should encourage us greatly that despite Jonah's rebellion God gives him another chance. Nor is this a rare occasion in Scripture. The God of the book of Jonah—indeed, of the entire Bible—is the God of the "second time." Abraham also experienced this:

"God had called Abraham to be the father of the faithful, and his life was to stand as an example of faith to succeeding generations. But his faith had not been perfect. He had shown distrust of God in concealing the fact that Sarah was his wife, and again in his marriage with Hagar. That he might reach the highest standard, God subjected him to *another test*."[1]

94

Jacob, too, knew God's grace in multiple manifestations. He experienced it during a night of deepest despair as he tried to escape the wrath of his brother Esau after cheating him from the birthright blessing:

"The evening of the second day found him far away from his father's tents. He felt that he was an outcast, and he knew that all this trouble had been brought upon him by his own wrong course. The darkness of despair pressed upon his soul, and he hardly dared to pray. But he was so utterly lonely that he felt the need of protection from God as he had never felt it before. With weeping and deep humiliation he confessed his sin, and entreated for some evidence that he was not utterly forsaken. . . .

"*But God did not forsake Jacob. His mercy was still extended to His erring, distrustful servant.* The Lord compassionately revealed just what Jacob needed—a Saviour."[2] And God granted him the vision of the heavenly ladder filled with angels.

After King David's adultery with Bathsheba, God sent the prophet Nathan to him, which brought the king a deeper experience of God's grace:

"The prophet's rebuke touched the heart of David; conscience was aroused; his guilt appeared in all its enormity. His soul was bowed in penitence before God. With trembling lips he said, 'I have sinned against the Lord.' . . . And the fifty-first psalm is an expression of David's repentance, when the message of reproof came to him from God. . . .

"David's repentance was sincere and deep. There was no effort to palliate his crime. No desire to escape the judgments threatened, inspired his prayer. But he saw the enormity of his transgression against God; he saw the defilement of his soul; he loathed his sin. It was not for pardon only that he prayed, but for purity of heart. . . .

"Though David had fallen, the Lord lifted him up. He was now more fully in harmony with God and in sympathy with his fellow men than before he fell."[3]

In the New Testament, the night Peter betrayed Jesus was the occasion for Peter's conversion and a new experience of divine grace:

"The sight of that pale, suffering face, those quivering lips, that look of compassion and forgiveness, pierced his heart like an arrow. Conscience was aroused. . . . Unable longer to endure the scene, he rushed, heartbroken, from the hall.

"He pressed on in solitude and darkness. . . . At last he found himself in Gethsemane. The scene of a few hours before came vividly to his mind. . . . On the very spot where Jesus had poured out His soul in agony to His Father, Peter fell upon his face, and wished that he might die."[4]

After the resurrection, at the Sea of Galilee, Jesus drew from Peter the assurance of his love and loyalty, for Peter had denied Him three times. "Before the assembled disciples Jesus revealed the depth of Peter's repentance, and showed how thoroughly humbled was the once boasting disciple. . . . The close, testing questions of the Lord had not called out one forward, self-sufficient reply; and because of his humiliation and repentance, Peter was better prepared than ever before to act as shepherd to the flock."[5]

Many had regarded Mary, the sister of Martha, as a great sinner, but Christ knew all the circumstances that had shaped her life, and He repeatedly forgave her:

"He might have extinguished every spark of hope in her soul, but He did not. It was He who had lifted her from despair and ruin. Seven times she had heard His rebuke of the demons that controlled her heart and mind. She had heard His strong cries to the Father in her behalf. She knew how offensive is sin to His unsullied purity, and in His strength she had overcome.

"When to human eyes her case appeared hopeless, Christ saw in Mary capabilities for good. . . . The plan of redemption has invested humanity with great possibilities, and in Mary these possibilities were to be realized. Through His grace she became a partaker of the divine nature. The one who had fallen, and whose mind had been the habitation of demons, was brought very near to the Saviour in fellowship and ministry. It was Mary who sat at His feet and learned of Him. It was Mary who poured upon His head the precious anointing oil, and bathed His feet with her tears. Mary stood beside the cross, and followed Him to the sepulcher. Mary was first at the tomb after His resurrection. It was Mary who first proclaimed a risen Saviour."[6]

The apostle Paul never forgot how God had pursued him while he was still a murderer:

"While so engaged as I was journeying to Damascus with the authority and commission of the chief priests, at midday, O King, I saw on the way a light from heaven, brighter than the sun, shining all around me and those who were journeying with me. And when we had all fallen to the ground, I heard a voice saying to me in the Hebrew dialect, 'Saul, Saul, why are you persecuting Me? *It is hard for you to kick against the goads'*" (Acts 26:12-14).

If we are truly honest with ourselves, we will have to admit that God has been even more gracious and forgiving with us than just the two times we have seen in Jonah's life. And when we aren't so focused on the sins of others and the work that God needs to do in their lives, we just might become more sensitive to how many times the Lord has extended His grace to us.

"Jesus knows the circumstances of every soul. You may say, I am sinful, very sinful. You may be; but the worse you are, the more you need Jesus. He turns no weeping, contrite one away. He does not tell to any all that He might reveal, but He bids every trembling soul take courage. Freely will He pardon all who come to Him for forgiveness and restoration."[7]

In the book of Jonah we see that God freely gives such grace to His recalcitrant prophet. He comes to Jonah the second time and repeats His original instructions. Nineveh is still the metropolis God wants him to reach. God will not let the impudence of His prophet frustrate His plans. Nor will He allow Jonah to wander off course. In fact, the prophet's second commissioning is even more explicit than the first as God urges, "Proclaim to it the message that I tell you" (Jonah 3:2, NRSV).

This time "Jonah arose and went to Nineveh according to the word of the Lord" (verse 3a). As in Jonah 1:3, Jonah "got up" and went. But this time, instead of trying to flee "from the presence of the Lord" (as pointedly noted three times in chapter 1), the text reports that Jonah obeys "according to the word of the Lord." "This time he did not stop to question or doubt, but obeyed unhesitatingly."[8]

In keeping with the writer's concise narrative style, Scripture mentions nothing of Jonah's long journey this time. The author had a reason for the detailed description of the prophet's first travels in chapter 1. It was to depict the extreme nature of Jonah's rebellion against God. But now, in chapter 3, Nineveh immediately comes into view—a typical feature of biblical narratives. For example, Genesis 22 gives no details of Abraham and Isaac's three-day journey to Mount Moriah. Instead, the text mentions only their arrival to the mountain of sacrifice "on the third day" (Gen. 22:4).

Biblical narrative writing omits many details that modern writers might normally deem important. Consider how Scripture rarely informs us of a person's physical appearance or what they wear. Such information appears only if it is vital to the outcome of the narrative. For example, of all the clothing Jacob's sons would have worn, the Genesis narratives mentions only Joseph's coat from his father because it will trigger the jealousy and the deception of his brothers. Later, Absalom's long and thick hair, specifically described by the narrator, will become the instrument of his death. Starkness of detail and few if any embellishments characterize most biblical narratives. This trait serves to give added weight to what the writer does mention. Thus the contrast in the amount of information provided between Jonah's first and second journey to Nineveh was deliberate.

Here is a good place to remind ourselves again about the intriguing literary nature of biblical narratives. We must reiterate that it is important to become sensitive to the sophisticated style of writing involved. The biblical writers did not intend their narratives as simple stories for children. And even if one cannot read the original language in which they were composed, we can become more perceptive to what the writers sought to convey by noticing what details they included, even if such particulars may seem unimportant at first glance.

In this specific instance, as we have seen, the author has omitted the details of Jonah's actual journey to Nineveh in stark contrast to his initial travels in the first two chapters. Instead, the writer directs our attention immediately to the metropolis of Nineveh, telling us that it "was an exceedingly great city, a three days' walk" (Jonah 3:3b, NASB). The account describes the city in the superlative degree, the verb following the subject in the original language, another way of giving emphasis in Hebrew. The literal reading of the phrase is "a great city to God," for God Himself pronounces Nineveh as "great."

Scripture designates only two cities in Israel as "great": Jerusalem (Jer. 22:8) and Gibeon (Joshua 10:2), neither of which was very large by modern standards. The adjective "great" sometimes can refer to a city's royal status.

Even so, archaeologists have found that Nineveh was large for its time. The emphasis on its "greatness" here in the book of Jonah may also include its importance as a religious center. It had "temples dedicated to the gods Nabu, Assur, Adad and Ninurta, in addition to Ishtar of Nineveh and others."[9]

In both chapters 1 and 3 of the book of Jonah God refers to Nineveh as a "great city." Not only is it an impressive city, but it is also "great" to God in light of all the trouble He takes to get Jonah there preaching!

The final phrase in Nineveh 4:3—"a three days' walk"—also suggests the size of the Assyrian capital. The words there are in apposition, thus reading literally "a three-day-journey city." Wiseman mentions that such a designation in ancient records can suggest a day's journey in from the suburbs, one day for business, and one day for the return.[10] Such an interpretation fits well with Jonah 3:4a, which describes the prophet fulfilling his divine commission: "Then Jonah began to go through the city one day's walk" (NASB). He went right into the city to proclaim his message.

Prophets are not strangers to city ministries. For example, God sent Elijah to the palace of the king in Samaria, the capital of the kingdom of Israel:

"To Elijah was entrusted the mission of delivering to Ahab Heaven's message of judgment. He did not seek to be the Lord's messenger; the word of the Lord came to him. And jealous for the honor of God's cause, he did not hesitate to obey the divine summons, though to obey seemed to invite swift destruction at the hand of the wicked king. The prophet set out at once and traveled night and day until he reached Samaria. At the palace he solicited no admission, nor waited to be formally announced. Clad in the coarse garments usually worn by the prophets of that time, he passed the guards, apparently unnoticed, and stood for a moment before the astonished king.

"Elijah made no apology for his abrupt appearance. A Greater than the ruler of Israel had commissioned him to speak; and lifting his hand toward heaven, he solemnly affirmed by the living God that the judgments of the Most High were about to fall upon Israel. . . .

"It was only by the exercise of strong faith in the unfailing power of God's Word that Elijah delivered his message. Had he not possessed implicit confidence in the One whom he served, he would never have appeared before Ahab." [11]

The Lord also dispatched his successor Elisha to Samaria (2 Kings 6:24–7:20). Jeremiah received a divine mandate to warn Jerusalem of its destruction:

"For forty years Jeremiah was to stand before the nation as a witness for truth and righteousness. In a time of unparalleled apostasy he was to exemplify in life and character the worship of the only true God. During the terrible sieges of Jerusalem he was to be the mouthpiece of Jehovah. He was to predict the downfall of the house of David and the destruction of the beautiful temple built by Solomon. And when imprisoned because of his fearless utterances, he was still to speak plainly against sin in high places. Despised, hated, rejected of men, he was finally to witness the literal fulfillment of his own prophecies of impending doom, and share in the sorrow and woe that should follow the destruction of the fated city." [12]

In the New Testament, Philip, the evangelist, went "down to the *city of Samaria* and began proclaiming Christ to them. . . . But Philip found himself at Azotus, and as he passed through he *kept preaching* the gospel to *all the cities* until he came to Caesarea" (Acts 8:5-40, NASB).

We also find Peter as a compelling witness to the Messiah in Jerusalem and Caesarea, the latter a prominent port city built by King Herod (Acts 10:1-24).

And we always encounter the apostle Paul in cities, teaching and organizing churches. He traveled to major thoroughfares of human culture, including those well beyond Israel. Ellen White writes of Paul's ministry that "in fulfillment of the commission given him by God, Paul had borne the gospel to the Gentiles, *he had visited many of the world's largest cities, and he was well known to thou-*

sands."[13] His vigorous ministry took him to such then-prominent cities as Galatia (1 Cor. 16:1), Ephesus (Acts 18:18, 19; 1 Cor. 16:8), Athens (Acts 17), Antioch (Acts 18:21, 22), and Corinth, where Paul not only worked but wrote to the church there two major Epistles.

"During the *first century of the Christian Era, Corinth was one of the leading cities, not only of Greece, but of the world.* Greeks, Jews, and Romans, with travelers from every land, thronged its streets, eagerly intent on business and pleasure. *A great commercial center,* situated within easy access of all parts of the Roman Empire, *it was an important place in which to establish memorials for God and His truth."*[14]

God directed Paul's ministry to the great city of Corinth with the poignant words: "Be not afraid, but speak, and hold not thy peace: for I am with thee, and no man shall set on thee to hurt thee: *for I have much people in this city"* (Acts 18:9, 10, KJV).

Ellen White, along with her counsel for families to live outside the city, also many times expressed her own deep yearning for the world's large metropolises. *"Night after night I am unable to sleep, because of this burden resting upon me in behalf of the unwarned cities.* Night after night I am praying and trying to devise methods by which we can enter these cities and give the warning message. Why, *there is a world to be warned and saved,* and we are to go East and West and North and South, and work intelligently for the people all about us. As we undertake this work, we shall see the salvation of God. Encouragement will come."[15]

"The Lord desires us to proclaim the third angel's message with power in these cities. . . . As we work with all the strength that God grants us, and in humility of heart, putting our entire trust in Him, our labors will not be without fruit. . . . *O that we might see the needs of these great cities as God sees them!* We must plan to place in these cities capable men who can present the third angel's message in a manner so forceful that it will strike home to the heart."[16]

"The time is near when large cities will be swept away, and all should be warned of these coming judgments." *"O that God's people had a sense of the impending destruction of thousands of cities, now almost given to idolatry."*[17]

It should not surprise us to find God directing Jonah to proclaim a message of judgment in the capital city of Assyria. However, it was at a time when other Israelites were no doubt praying for the Lord to overthrow the scourge of Assyria. As Philip Yancey mentions:

"Assyrians! The veritable Nazis of their day. This cruel, godless people, who razed whole civilizations and led captives away with hooks in their mouths, hardly deserved another chance. It was the height of insult to send him, a Hebrew prophet, to his archenemies. Who cared if Nineveh got destroyed in forty days; the more brimstone, the better." [18]

Instead we find God holding out His hand of mercy to the violent Ninevites.

A largely unexplored area in theology is God's relationship with all nations. His purpose in our world is vastly more extensive than just dealing with individual people, or even those who accept Him as their Lord. Ellen White tells us that "in the Word of God the curtain is drawn aside, and we behold, behind, above, and through all the play and counterplay of human interests and power and passions, the agencies of the all-merciful One, silently, patiently working out the counsels of His own will." [19]

Jesus describes His second coming as involving the whole world: "When the Son of Man comes in His glory, and all the holy angels with Him, then He will sit on the throne of His glory. *All the nations* will be gathered before Him, and *He will separate them one from another,* as a shepherd divides his sheep from the goats" (Matt. 25:31, 32).

God's intentions toward Nineveh should not be unexpected!

---

[1] E. G. White, *Patriarchs and Prophets,* p. 147. (Italics supplied.)

[2] *Ibid.,* p. 183. (Italics supplied.)

[3] *Ibid.,* pp. 722-726.

[4] White, *The Desire of Ages,* p. 713.

[5] *Ibid.,* p. 812.

[6] *Ibid.,* p. 568.

[7] *Ibid.*

[8] White, *Prophets and Kings,* pp. 269, 270.

[9] Donald J. Wiseman, "Jonah's Nineveh," *Tyndale Bulletin* 30 (1979): 36.

[10] *Ibid.,* p. 38.

[11] White, *Prophets and Kings,* pp. 120, 121.

[12] *Ibid.,* p. 408.

[13] White, *The Acts of the Apostles,* p. 406. (Italics supplied.)

[14] *Ibid.,* p. 243. (Italics supplied.)

[15] White, *Evangelism* (Washington, D.C.: Review and Herald Pub. Assn., 1946), p. 62. (Italics supplied.)

[16] *Ibid.,* p. 38. (Italics supplied.)

[17] *Ibid.* p. 29. (Italics supplied.)

[18] Philip Yancey, *I Was Just Wondering* (Grand Rapids: Eerdmans, 1989), pp. 61, 62.

[19] White, *Education* (Mountain View, Calif.: Pacific Press Pub. Assn., 1903), p. 173.

Nine

JONAH,
THE AMAZING EVANGELIST

Jonah has arrived in the city of Nineveh in Assyria. He now coura-geously proclaims the dire announcement of judgment that God has given him: "Yet forty days and Nineveh will be overthrown" (Jonah 3:4b, NASB). Picture the situation: in the capital city of Assyria a for-eigner suddenly appears and publicly pronounces doom on its busy streets. It could not have been an easy assignment for Jonah. But then the prophetic role has always been a hard one. And prophets have never coveted it.

It is critical to notice the content of Jonah's proclamation. God did not send him to lecture on monotheism or to urge higher ethical behavior in Nineveh, even though they would have been valid issues to raise with the Assyrians at that time. Nor had God commissioned the prophet to seek ecumenical unity. Jonah's pronouncement was that of judgment. And Nineveh had only 40 days of probation.

As we do further intertextual work, we notice that Scripture often associates the number 40 with periods of special significance. It is the number of days that rain covered the whole earth during the Flood (Gen. 7:17; 8:6) and the number of years that Moses stayed in Midian after fleeing Egypt (Acts 7:29, 30). Later Moses stayed on the "moun-tain of God" [Sinai] two different times of 40 days each (Ex. 24:18; 34:28; Deut. 10:10). The Israelites wandered in the wilderness 40 years after they rebelled (Ex. 16:35; Num. 14:33, 34; Deut. 1:1-3; 2:7; 8:2, 4). David and Solomon each reigned 40 years. Elijah's journey to Horeb when fleeing Jezebel took 40 days (1 Kings 19:8). And Christ's temptation in the wilderness at the beginning of His ministry lasted 40 days (Matt. 4:2; Mark 1:13; Luke 4:2).

Scripture connects the span of 40 days with the establishment of the covenant, for it is the number of days between the time when Israel left Egypt and when God gave them His law and covenant on Sinai. In the New Testament Jesus' glorified presence remained on earth 40 days before His ascension to heaven and inauguration as our high priest (Acts 1:3; cf. 2:33, 34; Heb. 3:17).

Jonah announces that Nineveh has been allowed "forty days" until their judgment falls. In his oracle he uses the verb "overthrown/overturn." More intertextual comparisons reveal that the choice of this verb in the book of Jonah is significant for two reasons:

1. Genesis 19:21, 25 uses this precise verb of Sodom and Gomorrah. In fact, Scripture employs two related nouns, both also meaning "to overthrow," almost exclusively of Sodom and Gomorrah when it mentions the two cities as experiencing God's judgment.

2. The verb also has a double meaning. We could translate the phrase as "Nineveh will be turned upside down," implying a dramatic change for the better, as happens in the book of Esther when it describes the Jews' deliverance from Haman's deadly decree:

"As the days wherein the Jews rested from their enemies, and the month which was *turned* unto them from sorrow to joy, and from mourning into a good day: that they should make them days of feasting and joy, and of sending portions one to another, and gifts to the poor" (Esther 9:22, KJV).

Jonah apparently broadcasts the striking message in Nineveh unflinchingly. It is clear that the city's inhabitants heard him, for the narrative describes the astonishing result: "So the people of Nineveh believed God, they proclaimed a fast, and put on sackcloth, from the greatest to the least" (Jonah 3:5).

The phrase "from the greatest to the least" (literally "from the great ones to the little ones") is a merism, a common Hebrew way to express totality by pairing opposites. For example: "The rich and the poor have this in common: the Lord is the maker of them all" (Prov. 22:2). Thus the book of Jonah makes us aware that the entire city of wicked Gentiles accepts what Jonah says as the truth. As we saw with the pagan sailors of chapter 1, here again in chapter 4 other non-Israelites, this time Assyrians, turn to the God of heaven. The notoriously wicked citizenry of Nineveh accept Jonah's words with all seriousness. They believe he is proclaiming a divine message.

In fact, the text pointedly states that "the people of Nineveh believed God." They don't believe just the prophet Jonah—they believe *God!* Thus Scripture pointedly instructs us that worshipers of other gods will respond to the one true God when confronted with His Word. Not only that, in this case the Ninevites accept that the threatened judgment is deserved and thus repent. Under conviction they exhibit the outward signs of repentance: wearing sackcloth and fasting. Such self-humiliation was their means of expressing submission to Jonah's God.

This reminds us that each person has a conscience stamped with the knowledge of a holy God. Paul, the apostle to the Gentiles, underscores this:

"For the wrath of God is revealed from heaven against all ungodliness and unrighteousness of men who suppress the truth in unrighteousness, because that which is known about God is evident within them; for God made it evident to them. For since the creation of the world His invisible attributes, His eternal power and divine nature, have been clearly seen, being understood through what has been made, so that they are without excuse" (Rom. 1:18-20, NASB).

Who would have expected that Jonah should meet with such an incredible reception from a violent population such as that of Nineveh? No evangelist could ask for a better response. What modern preacher today wouldn't envy such results! It is one of the most amazing conversion accounts in all Scripture. Ellen White informs us that "the Spirit of God pressed the message home to every heart and caused multitudes to tremble because of their sins and to repent in deep humiliation."[2]

Surprise conversions are not totally unheard-of in Scripture. Christians in the New Testament were truly shocked when they learned that Saul the persecutor had become one of them. Even Ananias, when God urged him to visit Saul, was so worried that he felt he needed to remind God just who Saul of Tarsus really was and what he had been doing to believers (Acts 9:13, 14)!

Here in the Old Testament we find another startling conversion story. This time it involves the entire capital city of the menacing country of Assyria. Even the royalty responded. "When the word reached the king of Nineveh, he arose from his throne, laid aside his robe from him, covered himself with sackcloth and sat on the ashes" (Jonah 3:6, NASB).

The "king of Nineveh" could have also been called the "king of Assyria." At that time the name of a chief city could stand for a country, even in written documents. We see this in 1 Kings 21:1, which mentions Ahab, king of Israel, as "king of Samaria." Again in Amos 1:3, 4: "Thus says the Lord, For three transgressions of Damascus and for four I will not revoke its punishment. . . . So I will send fire upon the *house of Hazael* and it will consume the citadels of Ben-hadad" (NASB).

The book of Jonah never mentions Assyria by name. The four chapters focus specifically on the city of Nineveh. The author never allows our attention to wander from Assyria's capital. And in the city of Nineveh we find the king including himself in its inhabitants' supplication of God.

Another example of "mirror writing," an important literary feature in biblical narratives that we discussed earlier, it vividly underscores the king's striking response to Jonah's judgment message. Notice the pattern in Jonah 3:6:

"When the word reached the king of Nineveh,

    A he arose from his **throne,**

        B laid aside his **robe** from him,

        B' covered himself with **sackcloth**

    A' and sat on the **ashes"** (Jonah 3:6, NASB).

This literary structure highlights the extent of the king's repentance. He moves from sitting on his royal throne to sitting in dusty ashes, as stressed in the outer lines of the verse. The ruler also exchanges his regal robe for sackcloth, the material of mourning, as contrasted in the two center lines of the literary structure. This often-used literary device in biblical narrative writing alerts perceptive readers of the particular point the writer intends to convey, "hiding" the meaning and theology of biblical narratives in plain sight!

Notice, too, that the Assyrian ruler does not avail himself of modern techniques of denying guilt. He has been wrong and is honest enough to admit it. Far from considering himself apart from the general citizenry of Nineveh, the monarch acknowledges his own need to repent. He does not doubt that God has a right to be angry with Nineveh. And we find the pagan king repenting before the King of kings.

Ancient evidence indicates that officials at the royal palace at times received special delegates to Assyria, including foreign prophets. Thus it is not surprising that the king has learned of the judgment warning. Mention of the king on his throne in the book of Jonah may indicate that he received Jonah in an official audience.[3] What *is* remarkable is what the king then does:

"He issued a proclamation and it said, 'In Nineveh by the decree of the king and his nobles: Do not let man, beast, herd, or flock taste a thing. Do not let them eat or drink water. But both man and beast must be covered with sackcloth; and let men call on God earnestly that each may turn from his wicked way and from the violence which is in his hands. Who knows, God may turn and relent and withdraw His burning anger so that we will not perish?" (verses 7-9, NASB).

The king acts immediately. It is the third occurrence of the verb "to proclaim" in this chapter, the previous two appearing earlier in verse 2. The king, his nobles, and the entire city take the message of Jonah as a God-given warning. The city declares a state of emergency.

The mention of flocks and herds in the royal proclamation may suggest that the heralds from the king went beyond the city walls into the rural areas that then generally surrounded major walled cities. Nor would the fact that the decree included the cattle have seemed strange at that time. Ancient records of the Persians and Greeks recall whole armies with their horses and beasts of burden involved in mourning rituals.

Moreover, we find a fundamental rapport between human beings and animals all through Scripture. The concept that even the beasts are distressed because of the burden of sin in our world has scriptural warrant:

"Consecrate a fast, proclaim a solemn assembly; gather the elders and all the inhabitants of the land to the house of the Lord your God, and cry out to the Lord. Alas for the day! For the day of the Lord is near, and it will come as destruction from the Almighty. . . . How the beasts groan! The herds of cattle wander aimlessly because there is no pasture for them; even the flocks of sheep suffer [literally: "bear punishment"]. To you, O Lord, I cry; for fire has devoured the pastures of the wilderness and the flame has burned up all the trees of the field. Even the beasts of the field pant for You" (Joel 1:14-20, NASB).

The attitude of fasting that the king calls for in Nineveh is also significant. Forbidding the drinking of water underscores and emphasizes the desperate nature of the situation. The king urges the Ninevites to "call insistently/mightily to God" in prayer. And everyone is to dress in sackcloth, the garb of penitence. Joel, another Hebrew prophet, echoes the same sentiment:

"Yet even now, says the Lord, return to Me with all your heart, with fasting, with weeping, and with mourning" (Joel 2:12, NASB).

"Gird yourselves with sackcloth
And lament, O priests;
Wail, O ministers of the altar!
Come, *spend the night in sackcloth*
O ministers of my God,
For the grain offering and the drink offering
Are withheld from the house of your God.
Consecrate a fast,
Proclaim a solemn assembly;
Gather the elders
And *all the inhabitants of the land*
To the house of the Lord your God,
And *cry out to the Lord.*
Alas for the day!
For the day of the Lord is near,
And it will come as destruction from the Almighty" (Joel 1:13-15, NASB).

The wearing of sackcloth reflects the wearer's recognition of the bankrupt state that sin leads to. The coarseness of the material depicts the ugliness of transgression. The fabric also represents how a sinner appears in the presence of a holy God. Ashes suggest the divine judgment fire that consumes, and what the ultimate end of sin will be.

The king further entreats each person in Nineveh to "turn from his evil way and from the violence that is in his hands" (Jonah 3:8b). Of the whole catalog of horrifying evils that one could have cited against the Ninevites, the king himself singles out violence. Violence was so characteristic of Assyrian culture that even the king feels compelled to mention it. As we noted earlier, it was especially their atrocities in war that the Assyrians wanted recorded on stone murals to depict their military might.

The king also insists that no superficial or vague confession of wrongdoing will be adequate. It must be accompanied by a change of behavior. In the original language the nouns precede the verbs at the beginning of the edict. Now the verb appears first. This striking syntax indicates the idea of insistence. "Let us put on" is the English equivalent.

The noun the king now employs includes meanings of evil, disaster, violence, and all the unjust behavior that promotes violence. Biblical prophets write in a similar manner. Amos declares: "They do not know how to do right, says the Lord, those who store up violence and robbery in their strongholds" (Amos 3:10, NRSV).

God also speaks just as plainly to the nation of Edom: "For the slaughter and violence done to your brother Jacob, shame shall cover you, and you shall be cut off forever" (Obadiah 10, NRSV).

The king of Nineveh honestly acknowledges the violent nature of his citizenry. But he now adds an urgent question: "Who knows? Who knows if God might be merciful?" The ruler realizes that the enormity of their sin might hinder God from forgiving them. And yet, He just might be merciful.

Nineveh's pagan king is as perceptive as was the sea captain in chapter 1 when he implored Jonah to pray during the storm: "Arise, call on your god; *perhaps your God will consider us, so that we may not perish*" (Jonah 1:6b). King David similarly hopes for the mercy of God when the child born of his adultery with Bathsheba becomes dangerously ill:

"Then his servants said to him, 'What is this thing that you have done? While the child was alive, you fasted and wept; but when the child died, you arose and ate food.' He said, 'While the child was still alive, I fasted and wept; for I said, *"Who knows, the Lord may be gra-*

cious to me, that the child may live"'" (2 Sam. 12:21, 22, NASB).

Who knows what the heart of the great God of heaven and earth may decide? Although Jonah's proclamation stirs the whole city to repentance, that will not in itself avert the promised judgment unless God changes His mind and extends mercy.

The people of Israel knew that the Lord responded when they truly repented. In fact, Moses had used the very words *turn* and *relent* in his intercession for the children of Israel at Mount Sinai:

"Then Moses pleaded with the Lord his God, and said: 'Lord, why does Your wrath burn hot against Your people whom You have brought out of the land of Egypt with great power and with a mighty hand? Why should the Egyptians speak and say, "He brought them out to harm them, to kill them in the mountains, and to consume them from the face of the earth?" *Turn* from Your fierce wrath, and relent from this hard to Your people.' . . . So the Lord *relented* from the harm which He said He would do to His people" (Ex. 32:11-14).

And God spared the idolatrous Israelites from their deserved judgment in His profound mercy.

Joel, a prophet in the same century as Jonah, called Israel to repentance with the same reminder of divine grace and mercy: "Who knows whether He will not turn and relent . . . ?" (Joel 2:14, NASB). The reigning monarch of the city of Nineveh now yearns for this possibility, but without daring to presume on God's goodness.

Right here in the book of Jonah we again encounter evidence of nations beyond Israel being aware of its God and His nature. Accordingly, the king's knowledge of Israel and its God should not surprise us. In an earlier narrative in the book of Joshua Rahab relates to the Israelite spies what her people knew about the Israelite nation:

"I know that the Lord has given you the land, and that the terror of you has fallen on us, and that all the inhabitants of the land have melted away before you. For we have heard how the Lord dried up the water of the Red Sea before you when you came out of Egypt, and what you did to the two kings of the Amorites who were beyond the Jordan, to Sihon and Og, whom you utterly destroyed. When we heard it, our hearts melted and no courage remained in any man any longer because of you; *for the Lord your God, He is God in heaven above and on earth beneath"* (Joshua 2:9-11, NASB).

The Jonah narrative confronts us with an additional striking comparison between God's own people and the pagan Ninevites. To the dismay of the prophets, Israel's attitude was ultimately unresponsive to God's pleas for repentance and a turning away from sin. As Hosea records:

"When I would restore the fortunes of my people, when I would heal Israel, the corruption of Ephraim is revealed, and the wicked deeds of Samaria. . . . Israel's pride testifies against him; yet they do not return to the Lord their God, or seek Him, for all this" (Hosea 7:1-10, NRSV).

Yet the pagan city of Nineveh at this time bows in abject repentance. Later, however, Nineveh does finally fall. Before that final judgment, however, God sends a second prophet to confront Nineveh with their wickedness, as we noted earlier:

"An oracle concerning Nineveh. The book of the vision of
    Nahum of Elkosh.
A jealous and avenging God is the Lord,
the Lord is avenging and wrathful;
the Lord takes vengeance on his adversaries
and rages against his enemies.
The Lord is slow to anger but great in power,
and the Lord will by no means clear the guilty. . . .
Your shepherds are asleep,
O king of Assyria;
your nobles slumber.
Your people are scattered on the mountains
with no one to gather them.
There is no assuaging your hurt,
your wound is mortal.
All who hear the news about you clap their hands over you.
For who has ever escaped your endless cruelty?" (Nahum
    1:1–3:19, NRSV).

Nineveh was a prominent pagan city. Yet God did not send Jonah to confront the physical or intellectual idols of that society. Instead, the Lord commissioned him to deliver a stark message of judgment. And the result was astonishing: "Then God saw their works, that they turned from their evil way; and God relented from the disaster that He had said He would bring upon them, and He did not do it" (Jonah 3:10).

Yes, it is clear that God notices human wickedness. But even more astonishing, a holy God also marks any turning away from evil. The narrative text doesn't mention the fasting or the prayers as the reason for God's mercy. Rather, it records that "then God saw their works, that they *turned from their evil way*" (verse 10). The Ninevites did more than perform outward deeds of penance. They changed inwardly. They *were* "overturned"! They *"turned"* from their evil ways. Paradoxically, Jonah's prediction. Nineveh was indeed "overturned"! And God's purpose in the stark judgment message was accomplished, for it brought about a mighty conversion of the people in Nineveh.

To all human appearances it might have seemed that the Ninevites were long overdue for divine doom. Yet the readiness with which they responded to God's Word reveals that in spite of all the wickedness and violence into which they had fallen, at that time they were not ready for final judgment. The depth of their repentance was profound by any standard. Even Jesus mentioned it: "The men of Nineveh shall rise up in the judgment with this generation and condemn it, because they repented at the preaching of Jonah" (Matt. 12:41).

Jonah's own people, despite their special covenant relationship with God, ultimately failed to heed the many prophetic warnings sent to them, and they also finally experienced their promised judgment, as the prophet Amos makes clear:

"Hear this word that the Lord has spoken against you, O children of Israel, against the whole family which I brought up from the land of Egypt, saying: 'You only have I known of all the families of the earth; therefore I will punish you for all your iniquities.' Can two walk together, unless they are agreed? . . . A lion has roared! Who will not fear? The Lord God has spoken! Who can but prophesy? Proclaim in the palaces at Ashdod, and in the palaces in the land of Egypt, and say: 'Assemble on the mountains of Samaria; see great tumults in her midst, and the oppressed within her. For they do not know to do right,' says the Lord, 'who store up violence and robbery in their palaces'" (Amos 3:1-10).

Throughout Scripture God consistently deals without partiality with all humanity. He applies the divine standard of morality evenhandedly. The book of Jonah is but one part of the extensive biblical evidence. Ultimately both Nineveh and Jerusalem are destroyed.

However, it is remarkable and sadly ironic how much more trouble God has had with one of His own people in the book of Jonah than with the worst of the pagan world! James Edwards is right: "Tougher than the transformation of the unrighteous is the transformation of the self-righteous."[4]

This pagan response to the judgment warning from God is most intriguing. The willingness of the Ninevites to turn away from and forsake their evil ways is truly amazing. In fact, Jesus later condemns the skepticism of His own people by referring to the pagan Ninevites:

"Then some of the scribes and Pharisees said to Him, 'Teacher, we want to see a sign from You.' But He answered and said to them, 'An evil and adulterous generation craves for a sign; and yet no sign will be given to it but the sign of Jonah the prophet; for just as Jonah was three days and three nights in the belly of the sea monster, so will the Son of Man be three days and three nights in the heart of the earth. The men of Nineveh will stand up with this generation at the judgment, and will condemn it because *they repented at the preaching of Jonah;* and behold, something greater than Jonah is here'" (Matt. 12:38-41, NASB).

Ellen White makes a similar comparison:

"Christ during His earthly ministry referred to the good wrought by the preaching of Jonah in Nineveh, and compared the inhabitants of that heathen center with the professed people of God in His day. . . . As the preaching of Jonah was a sign to the Ninevites, so Christ's preaching was a sign to His generation. But what a contrast in the reception of the word!"[5]

The book of Jonah again and again forces us to face a stark comparison between those privileged to be in the covenant line and those supposedly "heathen." For example, Jonah 3:8-10 repeats two verbs in the context of both God and the Ninevites:

"Let each man turn" *[shuv]* (verse 8).

"God may turn about *[shuv]* and be moved to pity" *[nacham]* (verse 9).

"and God saw . . . that they had turned *[shuv]* . . .
so **God turned**" *[nacham]* (verse 10).

The "mirror writing" and verb repetition emphasize that the very thing God wants to accomplish is the deliverance of the Ninevites. For God knows something about the Ninevites that Jonah doesn't want to face:

"Nineveh, wicked though it had become, was not wholly given over to evil. He who 'beholdeth all the sons of men' (Ps. 33:13, KJV) and 'seeth every precious thing' (Job 28:10, KJV) perceived in that city many who were reaching out after something better and higher, and who, if granted opportunity to learn of the living God, would put away their evil deeds and worship Him. And so in His wisdom God revealed Himself to them in an unmistakable manner, to lead them, if possible, to repentance."[6]

It is unfortunate that the King James Version translates the verb in Jonah 3:10 to say that God "repented." This raises all kinds of unnecessary questions about God's nature. The verb *"nacham"* more accurately should be rendered "relent," reflecting divine compassion. And, indeed, the New King James Version captures this nuance and actually uses the word "relent." Relenting is what God in His mercy does for Nineveh. And the book of Jonah thus underscores and enhances the consistent picture of God's merciful nature all through Scripture.

Obviously the Assyrian records would not mention such an event. However, some have seen a possible allusion to the conversion of Nineveh in the monotheistic-type religious reforms instituted during the early reign of Adad-nirari III (810-783 B.C.).[7]

As we saw earlier, archaeological records underscore the fact that God was right to call Nineveh to repentance. He hadn't been mistaken in His judgment of their wickedness, nor in His estimation of their disposition toward repentance at that time. Jonah, one of the most impressive of Old Testament "evangelists," at last completes his assigned task. What a glorious ending to Jonah's mission! Who could ask for more? But the surprises in the book of Jonah are not finished yet.

---

[1] Gen. 19:29; Deut. 29:23; Isa. 13:19; Jer. 20:16; 49:18; 50:40; Amos 4:11.

[2] E. G. White, *Prophets and Kings,* p. 270.

[3] D. J. Wiseman, "Jonah's Nineveh," pp. 29-51.

[4] J. R. Edwards, *The Divine Intruder,* p. 96.

[5] White, *Prophets and Kings,* pp. 273, 274.

[6] *Ibid.,* pp. 265, 266.

[7] In Gerhard F. Hasel, *Jonah: Messenger of the Eleventh Hour* (Mountain View, Calif.: Pacific Press Pub. Assn., 1976), p. 47.

Ten

OFFENSIVE GRACE

*J*onah has completed a most successful preaching mission. He can now travel home, full of joy and thanksgiving for God's mighty power to change even the most violently wicked hearts. At least that is what we might expect. But the prophet will continue to amaze us.

All through the book of Jonah thus far the prophet has registered rather low on any scale of comparison with all of the pagans he has encountered. In the first chapter the mariners and their captain perceive the power of God in the sea storm and worship Him. The wicked Ninevites in chapter 3 respond in true repentance to God. Even the pagan monarch in Nineveh humbly submits to God's sovereign authority, recognizing that the Lord was not obligated to spare the city (Jonah 3:9). Jonah obeys God only after the most dramatic divine measures. And in chapter 4 we will see that he is still hostile. Yes, God has had far more trouble with His prophet than with the most profligate of the Gentile world.

"In the charge given him, Jonah had been entrusted with a heavy responsibility; yet He who had bidden him go was able to sustain His servant and grant him success. Had the prophet obeyed unquestioningly, he would have been spared many bitter experiences, and would have been blessed abundantly." [1]

The narrative style of chapter 4 contrasts sharply with the other three chapters. It consists almost entirely of conversation. The first chapter in the book of Jonah is straightforward historical narrative with only two brief dialogues. The second chapter presents Jonah's poetic prayer from inside the "great fish." The third chapter resumes the historical progression. Now, here in chapter 4, the narrative suddenly "slows down." We pause from following events through time and listen instead to two remarkable conversations between Jonah and God.

As we mentioned earlier, those who have thoroughly analyzed the stylistic features of biblical narratives have noticed that the dialogues included within such narratives are important features. The conversations usually include issues critical to understanding the narrative. We will find that this is certainly the case in the book of Jonah.

The previous chapters have contained snippets of conversation, such as the time the sailors and the captain talk to Jonah during the storm (chapter 1) and the time Jonah responds to the sailors (Jonah 1:8, 9). However, here in chapter 4 we find two dialogues between Jonah and God. And, as we might expect, they are laden with profound issues.

The chapter opens with an insight into Jonah's present disposition. The text uses strong language to describe the prophet's response to God's generous grace toward Nineveh: "But Jonah was deeply offended and furious" (Jonah 4:1, paraphrase).

The original Hebrew expresses God's unexpected mercy toward the city as being "a great evil" to Jonah. That which would have caused the Lord great pain—the punishment of Nineveh—would have pleased the prophet. But God's acceptance of the people's repentance makes Jonah furious. The phrase literally reads: "it was hot to him," or "it burned to him."

This particular verb occurs elsewhere in the Old Testament, giving us additional insight into the strength of Jonah's anger. The book of Genesis, in the story of Cain and Abel bringing their offerings to God, employs the verb describing Jonah's anger for Cain's reaction to God's accepting his brother's offering and not his:

"So it came about in the course of time that Cain brought an offering to the Lord of the fruit of the ground. Abel, on his part also brought of the firstlings of his flock and of their fat portions. And the Lord had regard for Abel and for his offering; but for Cain and for his offering He had no regard. So *Cain became very angry* and his countenance fell" (Gen. 4:3-5, NASB).

And ultimately this anger drives Cain to murder his own brother.

We find this same expression when Jacob and Laban quarrel:

"Then Jacob *became angry* and contended with Laban; and Jacob answered and said to Laban, 'What is my transgression? What is my sin that you have hotly pursued me?' " (Gen. 31:36, NASB).

Jacob's sons are also furious at the seduction of their sister Dinah, and again we encounter this forceful indication of anger: "Now the sons of Jacob came in from the field when they heard it; and the men were grieved, and they were *very angry"* (Gen. 34:7, NASB).

Moses' response against Korah's rebellion against God is equally intense: "Then Moses became *very angry* and said to the Lord, 'Do not regard their offering!' " (Num. 16:15, NASB).

We see the same emotion captured in Samuel's anguish when King Saul deliberately disobeys God: "Then the word of the Lord came to Samuel, saying, 'I regret that I have made Saul king, for he has turned back from following Me and has not carried out My commands.' And Samuel *was distressed* and cried out to the Lord all night" (1 Sam. 15:10, 11, NASB).

Thus we cannot overemphasize the intertextual comparison of words and phrases in biblical narratives as a valuable tool for gaining insight into the meaning of that term or phrase, as we have just done here in Jonah's case. Each situation employing this particular verb depicts powerful emotions, often coupled with drastic actions.

Jonah's bitter resentment appears immediately after the announcement that God has granted forgiveness to Nineveh (Jonah 3:10). The prophet has seen his preaching bring a citywide repentance of all classes of people. One would think that he would be overjoyed. But the Lord has not punished Nineveh, and it makes Jonah furious.

His reaction should shock us. The strong expression in the original language indicates that Jonah's bitter anger has welled up from the depths of his being. It is like a child throwing a temper tantrum. Jonah 4:1 vividly portrays Jonah expressing his "burning" anger as he falls into a rage. The "overturning" of Nineveh has greatly "upset" the petulant prophet. The issue for him is not so much *that* God changes His mind but *whom* He forgives. How can God possibly share His mercy with the corrupt Ninevites? Everybody knew the Assyrians' reputation, as the Old Testament historical records remind us.[2]

In fact, the Assyrians are never friends of Israel in the Old

119

Testament. God even uses them as His instrument to punish His people:

   "Woe to Assyria, the rod of My anger

   And the staff in whose hands is My indignation,

   I send it against a godless nation

   And commission it against the people of My fury

   To capture booty and to seize plunder,

   And to trample them down like mud in the streets.

   Yet it does not so intend,

   Nor does it plan so in its heart,

   But rather it is its purpose to destroy

   And to cut off many nations" (Isa. 10:5-7).

Because of Assyria's loathsome reputation, Jonah is convinced that God is not strict enough with His grace. He is much too free with His mercy. The Ninevites should suffer the consequences of their wickedness and violence. Divine forgiveness offends Jonah, and he is furious! Curiously, at least, the situation constrains him to pray. But his prayer is also revealing:

"He prayed to the Lord and said, 'O Lord! Is not this what I said while I was still in my own country? That is why I fled to Tarshish at the beginning; for I knew that you are a gracious God and merciful, slow to anger, and abounding in steadfast love, and ready to relent from punishing" (Jonah 4:2, NRSV).

It is Jonah's second recorded prayer. His first prayer (Jonah 2:1) welled up from a man trapped inside a "great fish." Now he is distraught with anger. However, both times, Jonah prays to justify himself: "Is not this what I said . . ." (Jonah 4:2a, NRSV).

Now for the first time Jonah actually acknowledges the reason he originally tried to evade his divine summons to Nineveh. He admits why he initially tried to flee from his responsibility. Jonah even confesses that he tried to escape to Tarshish, employing the very verb used earlier in Jonah 1:3: "But Jonah arose to *flee* to Tarshish from the presence of the Lord" (NRSV). And once more the author reminds the reader of Jonah's panic as he determined to avoid the divine call.

So now it is confirmed. By his own words, the great preacher admits that he has had absolutely no regard for the Ninevites. He is even sure he is right to react the way he does. By implication he even rebukes God for how He has dealt with the situation. Never mind that the people of Nineveh acknowledged their guilt and repented. In Jonah's eyes they still deserve divine punishment.

Jonah simply cannot come to terms with God's including the Gentiles in His mercy. He simply cannot grasp why the Lord should allow them to partake of the special gracious benefits Israel enjoys as His covenant people. The prophet has already given plenty of evidence that he knows his Bible. As we have seen, he fills his prayer in chapter 2 with phrases and concepts from the Psalter. Thus he is surely aware of God's promise to remove our transgressions "as far as the east is from the west" (Ps. 103:12) But he is convinced that such mercy should be funneled exclusively to Israel, God's chosen people.

Perhaps, when Jonah evaluated the situation in Nineveh, he remembered the destruction of two other wicked cites that God earlier punished because of their wickedness. As we noted in the previous chapter, the description of the fate of Sodom and Gomorrah uses some of the same vocabulary as the book of Jonah does for Nineveh:

"Then the Lord rained on Sodom and Gomorrah brimstone and fire from the Lord out of heaven, and He *overthrew those cities,* and all the valley, and all the inhabitants of the cities, and what grew on the ground. . . . Thus it came about, when *God destroyed the cities of the valley,* that God remembered Abraham, and sent Lot out of the midst *of the overthrow, when He overthrew the cities* in which Lot lived" (Gen. 19:24-29, NASB).

Or perhaps the prophet recalled the Flood, in which God specified the reason for the destruction of the world at that time:

"Now the earth was *corrupt in the sight of God,* and the earth was *filled with violence.* God looked on the earth, and behold, it was *corrupt;* for all flesh had *corrupted* their way upon the earth. Then God said to Noah, 'The end of all flesh has come before Me; *for the earth is filled with violence because of them;* and behold, I am about to destroy them with the earth'" (Gen. 6:11-13, NASB).

Yes, Jonah knew his Bible. His rejoinder to God in Jonah 4 even included the sacred reference to God's character from Exodus 34:5-7: "I know that You are a gracious and merciful God, slow to anger, and abundant in lovingkindness, One who relents from doing harm"

(Jonah 4:2). The adjectives that the prophet uses of God—gracious *(channun)* and merciful *(rachum)*—Scripture applies exclusively to God. The concepts form part of God's own declaration of His being to Moses when He replaced the broken tablets of the Decalogue following Israel's golden calf apostasy:

"The Lord descended in the cloud and stood there with him as he called upon the name of the Lord. Then the Lord passed by in front of him and proclaimed, 'The Lord, the Lord God, compassionate *[rachum]* and gracious *[channum]*, slow to anger, and abounding in lovingkindness and truth; who keeps lovingkindness for thousands, who forgives iniquity, transgression and sin'" (Ex. 34:5-7, NASB).

All through the Old Testament, including the book of Jonah, we find that God delights in proclaiming His mercy! He simply cannot confine His love to only select human beings. Many biblical writers echo this glorious sentiment. The prophet Jeremiah represents but one of many:

"The instant I speak concerning a nation and concerning a kingdom, to pluck up, to pull down, and to destroy it, if that nation against whom I have spoken turns from its evil, I will relent of the disaster that I thought to bring upon it" (Jer. 18:7, 8).

It was a constant refrain of all the prophets, including Hosea and Joel:

"'How can I give you up, Ephraim? How can I hand you over, Israel? How can I make you like Admah? How can I set you like Zeboiim? My heart churns within Me; My sympathy is stirred. I will not execute the fierceness of My anger'" (Hosea 11:8, 9).

"'Yet even now,' declares the Lord,
Return to Me with all your heart,
And with fasting, weeping and mourning;
And rend your heart and not your garments.'
Now return to the Lord your God,
For He is gracious and compassionate,
Slow to anger, abounding in lovingkindness
And relenting of evil.
Who knows whether He will not turn and relent
And leave a blessing behind Him" (Joel 2:12-14, NASB).

The other attributes of God mentioned in Jonah's prayer—"slow to anger" and "abounding in steadfast love *[chesed]*" (NRSV)—also belong exclusively to the character of the Lord all through the Old Testament. And of course, Jonah would have been aware of the striking fact that God had first proclaimed His great lovingkindness to Israel following its worship of the golden calf, a time when He might rightfully have forsaken them. Thus this revelation of God's mercy in Exodus 34 was especially meaningful to Israel.

We find, however, that it upset Jonah that God would share His wondrous attributes with an evil city such as Nineveh. He is highly critical of any universal application of the divine qualities of grace and lovingkindness. He thinks God should reserve them for the righteous. Judgment properly *should* be the destiny of the wicked. In Jonah's mind God is far too prone to forgive sinners.

Jonah sees God's deferral of judgment on Nineveh as a huge mistake. The prophet strongly disapproves of sharing the Lord's compassion with wicked and violent non-Israelites. And he presumes to govern God's world better than the Lord does, accusing and condemning Him for being like He is. The prophet dares to castigate divine mercy and scorn God's compassion. And finally, here in chapter 4, we realize that ultimately Jonah's real reason for running away from his divine commission has less to do with Nineveh's vile sinners than with God's merciful character.

The prophet apparently had never figured out that the wicked Ninevites were really no different than he himself. Both the Ninevites *and* Jonah were all rebellious sinners deserving punishment. Yet God had graciously decided to show mercy to *all* of them. Jonah was willing to accept such wondrous mercy for himself, but not for Nineveh. And so he begs: "And now, O Lord, please take my life from me, for it is better for me to die than to live" (Jonah 4:3, NRSV).

Later Jonah repeats the same phrase in verse 8, underscoring the depth of his despair. He would rather die than have God find it in His heart to forgive the wicked Assyrians.

"Once more he yielded to his inclination to question and doubt, and once more he was overwhelmed with discouragement. Losing sight of the interests of others, and feeling as if he would rather die than live to see the city spared, in his dissatisfaction he exclaimed, 'Now, O Lord, take, I beseech thee, my life from me; for it is better for me to die than to live.'"[3]

It is not the first time that an Old Testament prophet prays for God to take their life. Recall that when the people of Israel continued to make bitter complaints against God in the wilderness, Moses "said to the Lord, 'Why have You been so hard on Your servant? And why have I not found favor in Your sight, that You have laid the burden of all this people on me? . . . I alone am not able to carry all this people, because it is too burdensome for me. So if You are going to deal thus with me, please kill me at once, if I have found favor in Your sight, and do not let me see my wretchedness'" (Num. 11:11-15, NASB).

Even bold Elijah, after the dramatic Mount Carmel incident, also despaired when he learned of Jezebel's death threat. "But he himself went a day's journey into the wilderness, and came and sat down under a juniper tree; and he requested for himself that he might die, and said, 'It is enough; now, O Lord, take my life, for I am not better than my fathers'" (1 Kings 19:4, NASB).

However, Moses and Elijah had better motivations than Jonah now displays. Jonah just couldn't comprehend why God had extended Nineveh's probation. He simply couldn't appreciate the fact that "Nineveh repented, and called upon God, and God accepted their acknowledgment of Him. Forty years of probation was granted them in which to reveal the genuineness of their repentance and to turn from sin."[4] Nor did Jonah care that when Nineveh's doom had been averted, God's glory had been praised far beyond Israel's borders!

"As king and nobles, with the common people, the high and the low, 'repented at the preaching of Jonas' (Matt. 12:41, KJV) and united in crying to the God of heaven, His mercy was granted them. He 'saw their works, that they turned from their evil way; and God repented of the evil, that he had said that he would do unto them; and he did it not' (Jonah 3:10, KJV). Their doom was averted, the God of Israel was exalted and honored throughout the heathen world, and His law was revered. Not until many years later was Nineveh to fall a prey to the surrounding nations through forgetfulness of God and through boastful pride."[5]

God's merciful forgiveness of Nineveh has so embittered Jonah that he no longer wishes to live. How differently would he handle things if he were in God's place! And how ironic that the cause of his misery is the goodness and forgiveness of God that he, as a disobedient prophet, has presumed on and experienced so dramatically when the Lord saved him from drowning.

Notice how God's attention now shifts from Nineveh to Jonah as He patiently tries to instruct His errant servant. And Jonah's gracious and merciful God gently asks him a searching question: "Is it right for you to be angry?" (Jonah 4:4). In just three words in the original language God urges him to reconsider his rancor.

The Lord's response is surprisingly mild. He desires Jonah to come to his senses and see the childishness of his behavior—and He could not be more patient about it. Helping His stubborn prophet become a more mature believer seems to be one of His paramount goals, just as important to Him as was the salvation of Nineveh itself. This becomes highly apparent now that we have worked our way through most of the book of Jonah. God challenges His prophet to think about his reaction, to analyze his thinking. Gently He urges Jonah to consider that he might not be correct in his evaluation of the situation.

Jonah is not the first or only person in Scripture troubled by how God does things. Scripture records many others who experienced deep agony as they tried to wrestle with the Lord's dealings with them. The anguish of Job as he suffers is one example:
"And now my soul is poured out within me. . . .
I cry to you and you do not answer me;
I stand, and you merely look at me.
You have turned cruel to me;
with the might of your hand you persecute me" (Job 30:16-
21, NRSV).
Jeremiah, also, expressed his confusion as he considered God's ways:
"O Lord, you know; remember me and visit me, and bring
down retribution for me on my persecutors. . . .
Why is my pain unceasing, my wound incurable, refusing to
be healed?

Truly, you are to me like a deceitful brook, like waters that
fail" (Jer. 15:15-18, NRSV).

Even the book of Psalms contains much pain. Though Christians
are more familiar with the praise psalms, almost 75 percent of the 150
psalms contain themes of distress and protest. And yet the Israelites
sang these very words in worship. No other people have ever engaged
with God with the same fervor as the children of Israel did. All through
the Old Testament we find a rich tapestry of such encounters, displaying rage, despair, and anguish. The intensity of relationship with
God in the Old Testament seems irreverent or even immature to some
modern Christians. But perhaps it is more a matter of our own imma-
turity in our own relationship with Him. All through the Old
Testament we find that people did not have to deny reality when they
came to God. Nor do we find God ever chiding the hurting:

"a bruised reed He will not break,

and a dimly burning wick he will not quench;

he will faithfully bring forth justice" (Isa. 42:3, NRSV).

In fact, God consistently shows amazing respect toward the expressions of protest we find throughout Scripture, Jonah included.
God apparently values honesty in our relationship with Him.

Here in the final chapter of the book, however, Jonah is not in any
mood to discuss the fundamental issues of divine mercy from God's perspective. He refuses to acknowledge any possibility that he might be in
the wrong. And he shamelessly persists in justifying himself. As the dialogue continues we find him still rejecting God's grace toward Nineveh:

"Then Jonah went out of the city and sat down east of the city,
and made a booth for himself there. He sat under it in the shade, wait-
ing to see what would become of the city" (Jonah 4:5, NRSV).

The prophet chooses a vantage point from which to watch what
will happen to Nineveh. The word "city" occurs three times in this
verse, as if to emphasize that Jonah is still very much focused on the
outcome of Nineveh, hoping for its downfall to prove him right. One
more time we remind ourselves that the repetition of key words in
biblical narratives is a clue to what the writer seeks to draw the
reader's attention to. Ancient narrative writers didn't use italics or underlining to stress something as we do now.

Let us watch as Jonah sits down on the east side of the city. Even this late in the narrative we will find still more miracles and yet more surprises.

---

[1] E. G. White, *Prophets and Kings,* p. 266.
[2] 2 Kings 15-19; 1 Chronicles 5; 2 Chronicles 28; and Isaiah 7; 8; 10; 11; 36; 37.
[3] White, *Prophets and Kings,* p. 271.
[4] White, *Selected Messages* (Washington, D.C.: Review and Herald Pub. Assn., 1958), book 2, p. 149.
[5] White, *Prophets and Kings,* pp. 270, 271.

Eleven

A WIND, A WORM,
AND A PLANT

The disgruntled prophet has expressed his considerable anger about God's mercy to the wicked Ninevites. And God has simply asked him to reconsider the situation. Now Jonah sits under a booth he has built himself for shade from the searing Middle Eastern sun. The dialogue will continue. But first, God again exhibits His sovereign power, as we have seen Him do all through the book of Jonah:

"The Lord God appointed a bush, and made it come up over Jonah, to give shade over his head, to save him from his discomfort; so Jonah was very happy about the bush. But when dawn came up the next day, God appointed a worm that attacked the bush, so that it withered. When the sun rose, God prepared a sultry east wind, and the sun beat down on the head of Jonah so that he was faint and asked that he might die. He said, 'It is better for me to die than to live'" (Jonah 4:6-8, NRSV).

God prepares an object lesson for Jonah.[1] As the "great fish" in the Mediterranean had previously been, at this point a plant, a worm, and another strong wind become God's instruments. And as with the "great fish," they obey.

Verse 6 in Jonah 4 opens with the pointed phrase "The Lord God *appointed* . . ." In our continuing endeavor to do careful narrative analysis, we become alert to this repetition. It is the second of four occurrences of this verb in the book of Jonah. Each time the author uses it, God is the agent, underscoring His sovereign rule over nature and circumstances as He accomplishes His purposes. The Lord still has not given up on Jonah. While the prophet sits in the booth he built to await Nineveh's outcome, God causes a plant to grow and bring wel-

128

come shade to Jonah. Just as we noted with the "great fish" in chapter 1, again the writer isn't concerned to identify the species of plant precisely. The focus of the narrative must remain riveted on Jonah.

Jonah 4:6 describes Jonah's exultant joy—the first he has expressed in the entire book. Ironically, it involves a plant. Perhaps he felt reassured that God was with him, since He had provided shade from the burning desert sun. The prophet's focus now shifts from the city of Nineveh to his own well-being. But the plant doesn't last long, for "God appointed a worm when dawn came the next day and it attacked the plant and it withered" (verse 7, NASB).

God, who had "appointed" the plant just the day before, now directs a tiny worm or weevil to attack the plant. Thus in the early hours of the day, literally "at dawn," the plant withers and dies, leaving Jonah to feel the full impact of the sun's scorching heat:

"When the sun came up . . . God appointed a scorching east wind, and the sun beat down on Jonah's head so that he became faint and begged with all his soul to die, saying, 'Death is better to me than life' " (verse 8, NASB).

The deliberate repetition of the verb "appointed" with the plant in verse 6, the worm in verse 7, and the hot wind from the eastern desert in verse 8 emphasizes the fact that the sequence of events in chapter 4 is no accident. The sun is up now and the heat becomes intense. No doubt Jonah is aware of the potential seriousness of the situation. Sunstroke is a real possibility and capable of causing death. However, the text indicates that Jonah suffers more acutely from his disposition than he does from the severe heat.

We need to pause and take a closer look at Jonah's attitude. In his initial conversation with God in this chapter, he protests the Lord's merciful nature: "I knew that You are a gracious and compassionate God, slow to anger and abundant in lovingkindness, and one who relents concerning calamity" (verse 2, NASB).

From Jonah's point of view, God was being unreasonable. Nineveh deserves judgment and punishment. Its cruelty was notorious. How could God possibly spare them from the fate that the prophet had been told to predict? Jonah is passionate about God punishing the city's disobedience, but apparently still oblivious to his own.

In verses 6 through 8 Jonah forgets all about Nineveh and becomes preoccupied with himself. Just when he had begun comforting himself that God was providing for him, everything goes wrong. Having lost the plant that helped to make his life tolerable, Jonah lapses into despair. Perhaps he has really been obsessed with himself the whole time.

Jonah has been demanding destruction from God. So the Lord does just that, directly demonstrating in Jonah's life the effects of his own theology. God sends a worm and a wind, and Jonah's shade plant withers. The prophet's bitter response unwittingly reveals him caring more about the death of his little shade plant than about the fate of thousands of people. Now Jonah is so bitter that for the second time that "he begged with all his soul to die, saying, 'Death is better to me than life'" (verse 8b, NASB).

His twice-declared morbid desire to die implies a deep spiritual problem. And it is from this that God is trying to deliver him. In his last words in the narrative, Jonah continues, as he has from the very beginning of the book, opposing God.

But Jonah does not have the last word. Again God asks him a question. "Then God said to Jonah, 'Do you have good reason to be angry about the plant?'" (verse 9a, NASB) Divine questions keep gently prodding Jonah. For the second time the Lord asks him to face and to analyze his anger. Each time that Jonah snarls that he wants to die, God tenderly urges him to reflect about his negative attitude. The repetition of the wording of both divine questions draws attention to the prophet's persistent anger.

God keeps the pressure on Jonah, for He knows well the danger of human anger. The first time we find anger mentioned in Scripture is in the opening chapters of the Old Testament—the account of the first murder. "And in the process of time it came to pass that Cain brought an offering of the fruit of the ground to the Lord. Abel also brought of the firstborn of his flock and of their fat. And the Lord respected Abel and his offering, but He did not respect Cain and his offering. *And Cain was very angry, and his countenance fell.* So the Lord said to Cain, 'Why are you angry?' . . . Now Cain talked with Abel his brother; and it came to pass, when they were in the field, that

OHIO DISTINCTIVE SOFTWARE

6500 Fiesta Drive
Columbus, Ohio 43235
Telephone 614-459-0453

October 30, 2003

Dear Customer:

As a special promotion, we're pleased to offer the **World Book Encyclopedia** Knowledge Suite **4 CD-ROM** set for **only $20**, plus, if you like, we'll send an identical set to a friend for only **$10!**

World Book Encyclopedia – 4 CD-ROM set

Disc 1 · 2004 World Book Encyclopedia Standard Edition CD-ROM – Over 25,300 articles, more than

360-degree "bubble views", 5 homework wizards, plus a 225,000-entry interactive dictionary!

Disc 2: World Book Illustrated Atlas on CD-ROM – Discover the world – click on a region of the virtual globe, and this atlas brings it to life. Go "off the beaten path" for guided tours to remote, exotic areas.

Disc 3: World Book Encyclopedia of Science CD-ROM – Contains complete text from the 8-volume print set, plus the enhancements you would expect in a World Book multimedia product. It provides detailed coverage of astronomy, physics, chemistry, planet Earth, plants, animals, and much more.

Disc 4: The World Book American Reference Library CD-ROM – History & Documents (42 volumes), Constitution Reference Collection (19 works), The Founding Fathers (12 volumes), The Supreme Court (1000 landmark cases), Classics of Western Civilization (11 works), U.S. Congress (collection of 17 works), 110,000 pages of Presidential Papers, 12,000 quotes, plus 4 volumes of learning aids.

Windows 98/2000/NT/and XP compatible. **Satisfaction Guaranteed 100%.** Please order before December 31, 2003. Thank you.

Sincerely,

Stanford Apseloff, President

P.S. If you provide your email address with your order, we will send you a special "email only" offer.

Cain rose against Abel his brother and killed him" (Gen. 4:3-8).

The first anger recorded in the New Testament involves King Herod. And it drove him to order the murder of innocent children. "Then Herod, when he saw that he was deceived by the wise men, was *exceedingly angry;* and he sent forth and put to death all the male children who were in Bethlehem and in all its districts, from two years old and under, according to the time which he had determined from the wise men" (Matt. 2:16).

Scripture warns about the dangers of human anger:

"Whoever is slow to anger has great understanding, but one who has a hasty temper exalts folly. A tranquil mind gives life to the flesh, but passion makes the bones rot" (Prov. 14:29, 30, NRSV).

"Do not be quick to anger, for anger lodges in the bosom of fools" (Eccl. 7:9, NRSV).

Accordingly, God was trying to help Jonah acknowledge his anger. However, the prophet continues in his self-justification. The Hebrew wording reveals him forcefully insisting that he has a right to be angry—"even to death." So central was the hatred of the Assyrians in his mind that when he saw how they escaped their threatened destruction he obstinately ranted that he preferred his own death to seeing them live.

In the New Testament Jesus describes a similar attitude of selfishness in the elder brother in the parable of the prodigal son. The first-born son resented the joyous merciful reception given to his returning wayward younger brother, whom he referred to as "this son of yours" to his father.

"Now his older son was in the field, and when he came and approached the house, he heard music and dancing. And he summoned one of the servants and began inquiring what these things could be. And he said to him, 'Your brother has come, and your father has killed the fattened calf because he has received him back safe and sound.' But he became angry and was not willing to go in; and his father came out and began imploring him. But he answered and said to his father, 'Look! For so many years I have been serving you and I have never neglected a command of yours; and yet you have never given me a young goat, so that I might celebrate with my friends; but when this son of yours came, who has devoured your wealth with prostitutes, you killed the fattened calf for him'" (Luke 15:25-32, NASB).

Both Jonah and the elder brother of Christ's parable are preoccupied with vindicating themselves. They both are convinced they are correct in condemning the offer of mercy. In Jonah's case he protests bitterly against God. And for the third time in this chapter (Jonah 4:9b, along with verses 3 and 8) he reveals his acutely negative attitude by expressing a desire to die. Jonah's last word in the book is quite literally "death."

Rather than turning away from Jonah, however, God continues speaking to his stubborn prophet: "But the Lord said, 'You have had pity on the plant for which you have not labored, nor made it grow, which came up in a night and perished in a night'" (verse 10). In the original language we find the specific inclusion of the independent personal pronoun "you," something rare in Hebrew grammar. Its inclusion makes a statement more emphatic. In this case, its purpose is to prepare us for God's final words.

In verse 10 the Lord says to Jonah, "You feel pity for the plant." He uses the same word for both His and Jonah's attitudes. God seeks to help His prophet comprehend what is happening. Jonah grieved over the plant only because he missed its shade, which left him feeling sorry for himself. He had never invested any time cultivating the plant, helping it grow as a gardener does. God is suggesting that Jonah's attachment to the plant could not have been very genuine, since the plant only "came up in a night and perished in a night." He is trying to enable Jonah to recognize that his concern resulted only from self-interest.

We find further significance in the choice of the verb "perish" in verse 10, which brings to mind the earlier occurrences of the word in the narrative. We have already seen it in Jonah 1:6, 14, when the captain and the sailors expressed their anguish about dying. It appears again when the king of Nineveh uses it in his decree (Jonah 3:9). All of these people dreaded the possibility that they were going to "perish." Jesus uses the Greek equivalent in John 3:16, which speaks about the "perishing" of the whole world. The narrator trivializes Jonah's concern for the plant by contrasting it to the sudden and violent death of human beings. God then draws further comparison between Jonah and Himself: "Should I not be concerned about Nineveh, that great city, in which there are more than one hundred and twenty thousand persons who do not know their right hand from their left . . . ?" (Jonah 4:11, NRSV).

Another use of the emphatic personal pronoun sharpens the difference between the attitudes of Jonah and God. And the text strongly implies that though Jonah hasn't had the long-term devotion of a gardener for his little plant, the Lord God *has* been toiling unceasingly over His creation, including Nineveh.

Then God addresses Jonah with one last question: "Should I not be concerned about Nineveh?" (verse 11, NRSV). The Lord intends His ironic question to prod His prophet into a different frame of mind. God hopes that Jonah will finally realize that he is wrong in faulting Him for being merciful and gracious. The "great city" of Nineveh is important to the Creator. The book of Jonah has now used the word "great" seven times. God Himself has employed it three times in referring to Nineveh. The final verse of the book has God speaking of "Nineveh, that great city," just as we find Him doing as the book opens (Jonah 1:2). Thus His regard for the wicked city has "enveloped" the book. Although Jonah detested this "great city," it is the object of God's profound compassion.

The Lord even refers to the number of inhabitants in Nineveh. A population of 120,000 is unusually high for a city of this period, underscoring the city's prominence. The count probably included those who lived in areas adjacent to the walled city. With God Himself knowing the census, we are reminded again, as we were when the book of Jonah opened, that God is keenly aware of cities and the people in them. Throughout Scripture He continually insists that He cherishes all His human creation. In the final verses of the book of Jonah God reminds His prophet that Nineveh is precious to Him and has cost Him no end of concern.

In Jonah's mind the people of Nineveh are extremely evil. He sees it as good reason to despise the Ninevites. However, in God's eyes the city's wickedness has increased His compassion. As the book of Jonah closes, it reminds us again how much greater the mercy of God is than that of human beings. King David well understood this, and expressed it when he was facing divine punishment: "Let us fall now into the hand of the Lord; for his mercies are great: and let me not fall into the hand of man" (2 Sam. 24:14, KJV).

In the book of Jonah God Himself admits His deep-felt mercy: "Should I not pity Nineveh, that great city, in which are more than one hundred and twenty thousand persons who cannot discern their right hand and their left?" (Jonah 4:11). God doesn't even allude to the Ninevites' sincere repentance. Instead He mentions those He pities. And He urges Jonah to reorient his perspective by asking: "Shall I not provide salvation for these people who are in ignorance and error?"

This verse should have a profound impact on the reader of the book of Jonah. God based His judgment of Nineveh on their wickedness. In His final discussion with Jonah in chapter 4, however, He instead points to their moral ignorance. And in the book of Jonah we see God caring deeply for both an impenitent individual such as Jonah and the morally ignorant citizens of Nineveh. Both receive His great mercy. God's heart yearns for people. In the New Testament the apostle Paul hears God express the same sentiment:

"And the Lord said to Paul in the night by a vision, 'Do not be afraid any longer, but go on speaking and do not be silent; for I am with you, . . . for I have many people in this city'" (Acts 18:9, 10, NASB).

The expression that God uses to describe the Ninevites in the book of Jonah—of not being able to discern "their right hand from their left"—appears five times in the Bible. In each case it refers to the moral issue of deviation from the divine law and revelation. The same phrase "right hand and left hand" also occurs in Babylonian texts as a synonym for "truth and justice" or "law and order." [2] Thus the book of Jonah instructs us that the Ninevites lacked knowledge of God. And God graciously defers judgment for the sake of the morally ignorant, for those who did not understand. The same astonishing divine attitude also revealed itself at Calvary, when "Jesus prayed, 'Father, forgive them, for they do not know what they do'" (Luke 23:34).

In the book of Jonah God permitted His prophet to experience His judgment in the stormy sea so that Jonah might know firsthand what judgment is like. He also delivered Jonah from drowning quite apart from the issue of whether as a disobedient person he deserved to be rescued. Though he never acknowledged the fact, Jonah became a recipient of God's grace no differently than Nineveh did. We find the Lord forgiving both Jonah and Nineveh in His great mercy. This is one of the major themes of the book of Jonah. And it is at the center of the discussion between God and His prophet.

Nineveh finally was reduced to ruins in 612 B.C. because of its great wickedness and violence, as we learn later from the prophet Nahum's ministry. But the generation that heard Jonah preach experienced a wonderful deliverance, and the God of the Hebrews "was exalted and honored throughout the heathen world, and His law was revered." [3] The book of Jonah records one of the grandest events in the history of redemption!

---

[1] E. G. White, *Prophets and Kings,* p. 272.
[2] D. J. Wiseman, "Jonah's Nineveh," p. 40.
[3] White, *Prophets and Kings,* p. 271.

Twelve

ONE LAST
QUESTION

The narrative now draws to a close. And it is God who has the final word. He concludes His discussion with Jonah with a most thought-provoking question:

" 'Should I not be concerned about Nineveh, that great city, in which there are more than a hundred and twenty thousand persons who do not know their right hand from their left, and also many animals?' " (Jonah 4:11, NRSV).

The book of Jonah comes to a sudden halt with a probing question that remains unanswered. Scripture never informs us whether or not Jonah finally recognized his self-centered reception of God's favor while at the same time begrudging it to the pagan Ninevites. Nor does it indicate whether the prophet was ever able to comprehend God's generous mercy that so far surpassed his own idea of fairness. We are left wondering if the prophet ever appreciated God's forgiveness of the undeserving—of which he felt perfectly free to partake.

And what about the notion of concluding the book with a question? It is a most unusual ending for a book in the Bible. And it is a most surprising question at that. Some may feel that the book of Jonah stops too abruptly. However, there is no reason a book cannot finish with a question. Nor does it necessarily imply incompleteness. In fact, it might be one of the most effective ways of portraying the sharp contrast between Jonah's attitude and God's.

Other passages in Scripture also end with unanswered questions, representing a way that Scripture writers express profound truths. For example, in the New Testament:

1. Jesus had been addressing a crowd of people and His disciples

136

regarding what discipleship really involved. He had talked plainly about how it meant taking up a cross and giving one's whole life for the sake of the gospel. And then He asks, "For what does it profit a man to gain the whole world, and forfeit his soul? For what will a man give in exchange for his soul?" (Mark 8:36, 37, NASB). How do you answer that?

2. After He healed the man at the Pool of Bethesda, "the Jews persecuted Jesus, and sought to kill Him, because He had done these things on the Sabbath" (John 5:16). In response, Jesus speaks of His divine authority in a lengthy discourse. He then concludes with a question: "For if you believed Moses, you would believe Me; for he wrote about Me. But if you do not believe his writings, how will you believe My words?" (verses 46, 47). And His challenging question receives no response.

3. The first chapter in the letter to the Hebrews reminds the reader of the grand and glorious scope of God's plan of salvation. It then concludes: "How shall we escape if we neglect so great a salvation?" (Heb. 2:3).

Asking probing questions is one way Bible writers express deep truths. Accordingly we find a question at the conclusion of the book of Jonah. God tells the prophet, "I saved you, and you didn't deserve it. Can't I save somebody else who doesn't deserve it either?"

All through chapter 4 God has kept delicate pressure on Jonah by confronting him with questions, hoping he will reconsider his evaluation of the divine treatment of the Ninevites. Yet, in a book full of surprises, one of the most startling is the final question to Jonah. Perhaps the most unexpected part is the closing phrase. Note the last words of the final verse in the concluding chapter in the book of Jonah: ". . . and much livestock?" (Jonah 4:11). God presses Jonah, "And what about all the innocent animals?" And then the book of Jonah ends. That's it.

Maybe the inclusion of animals shouldn't really be so unexpected. Many of us get so wrapped up in our busy lives and routines that we forget how important the natural world is to the Creator. However, the concluding question in the book of Jonah pointedly reminds us that even the animal kingdom falls within the sphere of God's tender regard.

Christians have often ignored this important biblical perspective. But right here in God's final appeal to Jonah, the Lord Himself includes the animals. By God's having mercy on Nineveh, even the animals can be spared. And it alerts to the fact that God closely links redemption and creation. Many Christians may have a correct doctrine of salvation, but they often need a more comprehensive doctrine of creation. The human mind has only slowly come to link ecology with morality. We are often insensitive to this significant biblical connection until the pollution and poisoning of our planet affect us personally.

As we have already noticed, the book of Jonah throughout portrays the "Lord, the God of heaven, who made the sea and the dry land" (Jonah 1:9) as sovereign over all His creation. But this perception is not restricted to the book of Jonah. It is the oft-expressed sentiment of many Bible writers in both Testaments. All the created world is part of God's concern, animals right along with human beings. It includes even the heavens, as the apostle Paul makes clear in the New Testament:

"For by Him all things were created, both in the heavens and on earth, visible and invisible, whether thrones or dominions or rulers or authorities—all things have been created through Him and for Him. He is before all things, and in Him all things hold together" (Col. 1:16, 17, NASB).

Paul no doubt had in mind the many statements of God's heartfelt concern for His creation all through the "law and the prophets," for his thinking was saturated with the Old Testament. The very first expression of God's expansive affection appears right in the opening chapter of the book of Genesis:

"God saw *all* that He had made, and behold, it was very good. And there was evening and there was morning, the sixth day. Thus the *heavens and the earth* were completed, and *all* their hosts. By the seventh day God completed His work which He had done, and He rested on the seventh day from *all His work* which He had done. Then God blessed the seventh day and sanctified it, because in it He rested from *all His work* which God had created and made" (Gen. 1:31–2:3, NASB).

The prophet Jeremiah also highlights the intimate relationship between God and His creation, even during times of judgment:

> "Therefore thus says the Lord of hosts:
> 'Behold, I will refine them and try them;
> For how shall I deal with the daughter of My people?
> Their tongue is an arrow shot out;
> It speaks deceit;
> One speaks peaceably to his neighbor with his mouth,
> But in his heart he lies in wait.
> Shall I not punish them for these things?' says the Lord.
> 'Shall I not avenge Myself on such a nation as this?'
> I will take up a weeping and wailing for the mountains,
> And for the dwelling places of the wilderness a lamentation,
> Because they are burned up,
> So that no one can pass through;
> Nor can men hear the voice of the cattle.
> Both the birds of the heavens and the beasts have fled;
> They are gone" (Jer. 9:7-10).

When God speaks of judgment against sin, He includes lament for His created world.

The final book of Scripture again dramatically encompasses the entire created world within God's sphere of judgment:

1. Revelation 7:1 pictures four angels "holding back the four winds of the earth, so that no wind would blow *on the earth or on the sea or on any tree*" (NASB). Another angel joins them, having the seal of God and bringing the command, *"Do not harm the earth or the sea or the trees* until we have sealed the bond-servants of our God on their foreheads" (verse 3, NASB).

2. In Revelation 11, after the seventh trumpet sounds, the 24 elders fall on their faces and worship God, crying out against those who have wreaked havoc on the created world. "We give You thanks, O Lord God, the Almighty, who are and who were, because You have taken Your great power and have begun to reign. And the nations were enraged, and Your wrath came, and the time came for the dead to be judged, and the time to reward Your bond-servants the prophets and the saints and those who fear Your name, the small and

the great, and *to destroy those who destroy the earth"* (Rev. 11:17, 18, NASB).

From Genesis to Revelation, the Bible never allows us to forget the profound value that God places on His created world. The book of Jonah itself concludes with this issue.

According to Genesis 1 and 2, God created human beings in His image. Scholars have widely discussed what this involves. Surely it includes the understanding that we are to reflect His holy character by acting responsibly toward His creation, exhibiting careful regard for the earth and the animals since we know that it is what God Himself does. If we are to reflect His image on earth, we are particularly responsible for the quality of our relationships with all His creatures. God gave humanity dominion over the animals (Gen. 1:26-28). Thus we have divinely assigned responsibility for life in all its forms on earth, including the animals.

"The Creation story is about the nurture of life, which is . . . recognized in the task of humans to rule and to govern the animal world, and to guard and preserve the creation order (compare Genesis 1:28 with Genesis 2:15). These two texts are not in contrast, but related to each other. Rolf Rendtorff put it this way: 'Thus we learn that "master" in Gen 1:28 does not mean "subdue," as it is often rendered in English translations, but to work carefully and guard' ["What We Miss by Taking the Bible Apart," p. 44]."[1]

In light of this, it is important to remind ourselves that both human beings and animals have the same origin—from the hand of the same Creator. And He created all of us, humans and animals alike, as a "living soul." In fact, Scripture underscores many similarities between human beings and animals:

1. They were both created as *nephesh ha-ya* ("living beings, creatures") (Gen. 1:20, 24; 2:7, 19).

2. They were both blessed by God (Gen. 1:22, 28).

3. They both received a vegetarian diet (Gen. 1:29, 30).

4. They both have blood in their veins. That blood is a symbol of life (Gen. 9:4-6).

5. They both could be responsible for murder (Gen. 9:5; Ex. 21:28-32).

6. They are both a party to God's covenant (Gen. 9:9, 10).

7. They are both under the death penalty if engaged in bestiality (Lev. 20:15, 16).

8. They should both keep the Sabbath rest (Ex. 20:8-10; Lev. 23:10-12).

9. They will both live together in peace and will return to original conditions in the kingdom of God (Isa. 11:7-9; Hosea 2:18-20).

10. The firstborn from humans and animals belong to God (Ex. 22:29, 30; 13:12, 13).

11. Priests and sacrificial animals have to be without spot or blemish (Lev. 21:17-21; 22:19-25).

12. Animals could not be sacrificed unless eight days old, and then they were to be dedicated to God. The same time period of eight days was given for a boy to be circumcised (Lev. 22:27; Ex. 22:30; Gen. 17:12).[2]

In light of the close relationship between all created life, it should not surprise us to find that Bible writers consistently view animals as a significant part of God's world, and that He has specifically provided for their responsible care. For example, when God announces His covenant with Noah after the Flood, He explicitly includes animals as an important part of His covenant with the world:

"Then God spoke to Noah and to his sons with him, saying, 'Now behold, I Myself do establish My covenant with you, and with your descendants after you; *and with every living creature that is with you, the birds, the cattle, and every beast of the earth with you; of all that comes out of the ark, even every beast of the earth.* I establish My covenant with you; and all flesh shall never again be cut off by the water of the flood, neither shall there again be a flood to destroy the earth.' God said, 'This is the sign of the covenant which I am making between Me and you and *every living creature* that is with you, for all successive generations; I set My bow in the cloud, and it shall be for a sign of a covenant between Me and *the earth*'" (Gen. 9:8-13, NASB).

Paul goes even further by declaring that created things reveal to us the very nature of the Godhead: "Ever since the creation of the world [God's] eternal power and divine nature, invisible though they are, have been understood and seen through the things he has made" (Rom. 1:20, NRSV).

God repeatedly affirms through His prophets that His covenant involves all of the created order, and that ultimately He will restore the original perfection of creation:

"I will make for you a covenant on that day with the wild animals, the birds of the air, and the creeping things of the ground; and I will abolish the bow, the sword, and war from the land; and I will make you lie down in safety" (Hosea 2:18, NRSV).

"The wolf and the lamb shall feed together; the lion shall eat straw like the ox; and dust shall be the serpent's food. They shall not hurt nor destroy in all My holy mountain, says the Lord" (Isa. 65:25).

Paul instructs us that all creatures—both humans and animals— were made by and for Jesus Christ:

"For in him all things in heaven and on earth were created, things visible and invisible, whether thrones or dominions or rulers or powers—all things have been created through him and for him" (Col. 1:16, NRSV).

Their value derives from God's delight in them, and their purpose is to worship and serve Him (Gen. 1:31; Prov. 8:30, 31). His care covers all of His creation. God provides even for the sustenance of the animals: "He gives to the beast its food, and to the young ravens that cry" (Ps. 147:9). In fact, the psalms repeatedly refer to all spheres of God's creation:

"Praise the Lord from the earth,
   you sea monsters and all deeps,
   fire and hail, snow and frost,
   stormy wind fulfilling his command!
   Mountains and all hills,
   fruit trees and all cedars!
   Wild animals and all cattle,
   creeping things and flying birds!
   Kings of the earth and all peoples,
   princes and all rulers of the earth!
   Young men and women alike,
   old and young together!

142

Let them praise the name of the Lord,
for his name alone is exalted;
his glory is above earth and heaven" (Ps. 148:7-13, NRSV).

Both Old Testament and New Testament writers regularly remind us that animals have intrinsic value to God. Some Christian writers have seen that creation itself is grace, the result of the sheer generosity of God. In that light we would do well to pause in wonder, awe, and thanksgiving. Jesus Himself has reminded us that He notices what happens to what we might consider as rather insignificant creatures: "Are not two sparrows sold for a cent? And yet not one of them will fall to the ground apart from your Father" (Matt. 10:29, NASB).

Scripture also instructs us that because of the close intertwining of all aspects of the created world, human sin has affected the entire creation and it suffers the consequences. Paul poignantly writes:

"For the anxious longing of the creation waits eagerly for the revealing of the sons of God. For the creation was subjected to futility, not willingly, but because of Him who subjected it, in hope that the creation itself also will be set free from its slavery to corruption into the freedom of the glory of the children of God. For we know that the whole creation groans and suffers the pains of childbirth together until now" (Rom. 8:19-22, NASB).

The Bible promises that the animal kingdom will also participate in the restoration of Edenic perfection, for both the Fall and redemption always include the whole of creation. The prophet Isaiah waxes eloquent as he describes the righteous reign of Christ reestablishing justice and righteousness on the earth:

"And the wolf will dwell with the lamb, and the leopard will lie down with the young goat, and the calf and the young lion and the fatling together; and a little boy will lead them. Also the cow and the bear will graze, their young will lie down together, and the lion will eat straw like the ox. The nursing child will play by the hole of the cobra, and the weaned child will put his hand on the viper's den. They will not hurt or destroy in all My holy mountain, for the earth will be full of the knowledge of the Lord as the waters cover the sea" (Isa. 11:6-9, NASB).

Because of the close biblical linkage between creation and redemption, it is not surprising that biblical writers, when speaking of events in nature, consistently ascribe them to God. This has been apparent several times in the book of Jonah alone. God deals with just one single stubborn individual by deliberately "hurling" a storm to arrest Jonah in his flight (see Jonah 1:4, NASB). The author does not merely attribute the storm to the raw elements of nature. No, we cannot overestimate God's involvement in His created world!

"Forever, O Lord, Your word is settled in heaven. Your faithfulness continues throughout all generations; You established the earth, and it stands. They stand this day according to Your ordinances, for all things are Your servants" (Ps. 119:89-91, NASB).

"Praise ye him, sun and moon: praise him, all ye stars of light. Praise him, ye heavens of heavens, and ye waters that be above the heavens. Let them praise the name of the Lord: for he commanded, and they were created. He hath also established them for ever and ever: he hath made a decree which shall not pass. Praise the Lord from the earth, ye dragons, and all deeps: fire, and hail; snow, and vapor; stormy wind fulfilling his word" (Ps. 148:3-8, KJV).

In the New Testament, when the Lord Jesus walked on earth He continued to demonstrate His divine power over nature. We observe many examples:

1. Jesus' first miracle changed water into wine for a wedding feast (John 2).

2. The stormy sea knew His voice and obeyed His command (Mark 4:35-41).

3. Jesus walked on water (Matt. 14:25-27).

4. The fig tree withered under His curse (Matt. 21:18, 19).

5. A fish brought Him a coin (Matt. 17:24-27).

6. He vanquished disease, including the dreaded leprosy (Luke 17:11-21).

7. Even death could not remain in His presence (Luke 7:11-16; John 11).

8. The heavens, "at the sight of His dying anguish, [hid] its face of light."[3]

9. Even inanimate nature bore witness to His divinity: "The rocks [knew] Him, and had shivered into fragments at His cry."[4]

Ellen White follows in this same biblical tradition when she writes that "it is by the mighty power of the Infinite One that the elements of nature in earth and sea and sky are kept within bounds."[5]

God's creation delights to do His will. Only disobedient human beings resist Him. We have seen this clearly right in the book of Jonah. And yet the Creator, "the God of heaven, who made the sea and the dry land" (Jonah 1:9), has a tender regard for His erring children, "as well as . . . [the] animals" (Jonah 4:11, NASB). It really shouldn't be unexpected that He mentions the animals of Nineveh in His final question to Jonah.

The book then ends, as it began, with the word of God to Jonah, a human being that God obviously knows very well.

---

[1] Jiří Moskala, *The Laws of Clean and Unclean Animals in Leviticus 11: Their Nature, Theology, and Rationale (An Intertextual Study)* (Berrien Springs, Mich.: Adventist Theological Society Publications, 2000), p. 296.

[2] *Ibid.,* pp. 298, 299.

[3] E. G. White, *The Desire of Ages,* p. 771.

[4] *Ibid.*

[5] White, *Prophets and Kings,* p. 134.

Thirteen

WHAT'S IT
ALL ABOUT?

The book of Jonah, composed of four superbly written chapters, is an amazing account of the prophet Jonah. But is the main focus of this narrative? What was the purpose behind it? What was the author really trying to communicate? When people examine the story they usually pay a lot of attention to the "great fish." But surely that is not the primary point. After all, only three verses mention the sea creature.

The book gives no indication as to who might have written it. Second Kings 14:25, as we saw earlier, mentions Jonah as the "son of Amittai, the prophet, who was from Gath-hepher" (NASB). This can help to fit in a few more clues as to who Jonah was and when he lived:

"In the fifteenth year of Amaziah the son of Joash king of Judah, Jeroboam the son of Joash king of Israel became king in Samaria, and reigned forty-one years. He did evil in the sight of the Lord; he did not depart from all the sins of Jeroboam the son of Nebat, which he made Israel sin. He restored the border of Israel from the entrance of Hamath as far as the Sea of the Arabah, according to the word of the Lord, the God of Israel, which He spoke through His servant Jonah the son of Amittai, the prophet, who was of Gath-hepher" (verses 23-25).

The passage informs us that Jonah served during the reign of King Jeroboam II of Israel (793-753 B.C.). During the rule of his immediate predecessors the Aramean states headed by Damascus had made savage attacks on Israel, inflicting terrible suffering on the population (2 Kings 13:5; Amos 1:3). Jehoash (798-782 [793-782 coregency with Jeroboam II]) succeeded in recovering the cities of Israel (2 Kings 13:25), and Jonah apparently predicted that Jeroboam would restore

Israel's borders to their Davidic limits.

Second Kings 14:25-27 reports the fulfillment of that prophecy. Israel prospered once more—but not for long. Both Hosea and Amos severely rebuked the northern kingdom as early as the time of Jeroboam's reign (Hosea 1:1; Amos 1:1). But whereas Amos was a southerner from Tekoa, not far from Bethlehem, Jonah was a northerner. Perhaps his family had suffered during the Syrian incursions into Israel. If so, it might explain some of his antagonism to Nineveh of Assyria—an even more menacing country at that time than Syria.

Perhaps some of the lessons implied in the book of Jonah might also apply to the church. When God asked Jonah to go to Nineveh, the prophet initially refused. But Jonah finally realized that the Lord could not be deterred.

God has commissioned many individuals to deliver a divine message. He instructed Moses to go to Egypt and confront Pharaoh (Ex. 3; 4). Gideon, too, heard God's bidding: "Then the Lord turned to him and said, 'Go in this might of yours, and you shall save Israel from the hand of the Midianites. Have I not sent you?'" (Judges 6:14).

In the New Testament, after healing the demoniac Jesus bids him to "go home to your friends, and tell them what great things the Lord has done for you, and how He has had compassion on you" (Mark 5:19).

When Jesus sent out the 12 disciples out on their first missionary journey, He told them to "go . . . to the lost sheep of the house of Israel" (Matt. 10:6). After the Resurrection the angel urged the women who had come to the tomb to "go, tell His disciples—and Peter—that He is going before you into Galilee; there you will see Him, as He said to you" (Mark 16:7). Jonah's call fits into a well-established pattern in Scripture.

The apostle Paul's life stands in stark contrast to the prophet Jonah's reaction to his divine bidding. His response is quite different from that of the son of Amittai. Rather than trying to evade his responsibility, Paul makes three strong personal statements of conviction to the Romans, the inhabitants of another great capital city:

"*I am under obligation* both to Greeks and to barbarians, both to the wise and to the foolish. So, for my part, *I am eager* to preach the gospel to you also who are in Rome. *For I am not ashamed of the gospel,* for it is the power of God for salvation to everyone who believes, to the Jew first and also to the Greek" (Rom. 1:14-16, NASB).

Notice that Paul addresses the Romans not as a tourist but as an evangelist. Rome was a major pagan city of his time, a great center of imperial pride and power and probably a difficult place to witness in. Yet Paul speaks of his urgent obligation. Nor was his message to Rome a "warm fuzzy." The first issue he brings up to the Romans, as did Jonah to Nineveh, is God's wrath against sin.

Prophetic messages rarely involve an exclusive focus on a sentimental divine love. The very first sermon Peter preached after the climactic pouring out of the Holy Spirit was not "God is a God of love. That's all you need to know." Instead, we hear the disciple insisting, "Men of Israel, listen to these words: Jesus the Nazarene, a man attested to you by God with miracles and wonders and signs which God performed through Him in your midst, just as you yourselves know— this Man, delivered over by the predetermined plan and foreknowledge of God, you nailed to a cross by the hands of godless men and put Him to death" (Acts 2:22, 23, NASB).

Peter's sermon and Paul's declaration to Rome are in direct antithesis not only to Jonah's attitude but also to many in the church today who tend to regard Christ's great commission to the church as an option. And that they are doing God a favor if they engage in evangelism at all.

God has given the church an urgent command. He has told us to "go," just as He did Jonah: "And Jesus came and spoke to them, saying, 'All authority has been given to Me in heaven and on earth. *Go* therefore and make disciples of all the nations, baptizing them in the name of the Father and of the Son and of the Holy Spirit, teaching them to observe all things that I have commanded you; and lo, I am with you always, even to the end of the age'" (Matt. 28:18-20).

We should learn from Jonah's experience that we should not take the Lord's commands lightly. We too, like Jonah, need to learn to see the world from His eyes: "Men boast of the wonderful progress and enlightenment of the age in which we are now living; but God sees the earth filled with iniquity and violence."[1]

God has commissioned the Seventh-day Adventist Church to proclaim a judgment message as He did Jonah, so that "the great things of [His] law—the principles of justice, mercy, and love" may be set forth in their true light.[2] God is serious about this. Indeed, He is determined that His people will carry out the Great Commission, a fact that we can learn from Jonah's experience.

Perhaps we hesitate to proclaim such a stark judgment message. Maybe we, as did Jonah, find ourselves embarrassed that God's mercy has postponed the judgment we have preached about for so long. And like Jonah, "jealous of [our] reputation," we have "lost sight" of the "infinitely greater value" of people.[3]

It could be that as we have looked at the life of Jonah we have seen in those four chapters not just a depiction of a stubborn prophet, but even more important, we have recognized an unwelcome reflection of ourselves. How many of us have run away from God and His explicit instruction? A potential Jonah lurks in each of our hearts. What divine command do we not want to hear? What instructions from Him annoy us? What divine assignment causes us to resist? And what has prompted us to say, "Anything but that, Lord"? Have we ever found ourselves limiting God's mercy to anyone else? Do we even restrict divine mercy to ourselves?

Most of us have our own "cities" of escape and evasion. Perhaps our own "Nineveh" is some clear instruction of God's will for us. Or it might it be the Lord's urging that we change some aspect of our behavior, or carry out some directive that demands more than we want to give. How many of us hear the word of the Lord and go the opposite way until we too finally find out, like Saul of Tarsus, that it is "hard . . . to kick against the pricks" (Acts 26:14, KJV).

We readily notice others in the church that need correction. But, like Jonah, we are blind to our own problems. The fact is that even the finest among us—even the most highly gifted and educated—are sinners in need of God's mercy. "For all of us have become like one who is unclean, and all our righteous deeds are like a filthy garment; and all of us wither like a leaf, and our iniquities, like the wind, take us away" (Isa. 64:6, NASB).

"Because you say, 'I am rich, and have become wealthy, and have

JONAH

need of nothing,' and you do not know that you are wretched and miserable and poor and blind and naked" (Rev. 3:17, NASB).

And, in spite of all the good things we may do for the church, we need to learn to sing that great spiritual:

"Not my brother nor my sister, but it's me, O Lord,
standin' in the need of prayer."

The church needs more than natural abilities and intellectual brilliance. All of us, just like Jonah, must have God's special grace to give us love for the lost and fervor for His commission. Could it be possible that some within the Seventh-day Adventist Church no longer take seriously the proclamation of the final message of warning to a lost world? Perhaps some think we have such a monopoly on truth that our lack of zeal doesn't matter.

The book of Jonah thus becomes one of the most relevant books in Scripture for this time. It has a profound message to the church in the twenty-first century. Each of us needs to evaluate carefully whether or not we, like Jonah, are running in a different direction than God has set out for us. Are we traveling to Tarshish instead of Nineveh? Are we asleep while the world tosses in unprecedented confusion? Many in the world are apprehensive of the "coming storm," yet are we, like Jonah, asleep? God used the sea captain to wake Jonah up. What will He need to arouse us?

Sometimes one wonders: if the Holy Spirit withdrew from the church, would it even make a difference? Would the church merely continue on as though nothing had happened? Is Jesus sorrowfully asking us: "If you had known, even you, especially in this your day, the things that make for your peace" (Luke 19:42)? The narrative of the book of Jonah seems extremely contemporary, doesn't it?

"We would rather be ruined than changed
We would rather die in our dread
Than climb the cross of the moment
And let our illusions die."

—W. H. Auden

[1] E. G. White, *Prophets and Kings,* p. 275.
[2] *Ibid.*
[3] *Ibid.,* p. 271.

150

Fourteen

A PICTURE
OF GOD

The book of Jonah is superbly written. As in every biblical narrative, the issues it raises are profound, yet communicated subtly. Too often modern minds relegate biblical stories or narratives to nice little stories for childish reflection and only "secondary materials" when compared to the real theology of the gospel. Some assume that the Old Testament narratives provide pleasant reading but are not particularly valuable for deep theological reflection. However, the biblical authors did not pen their with children in mind. Biblical narratives are a highly sophisticated type of writing.

More and more people are appreciating this fact as our understanding of the depth of narrative expression increases. Biblical writers clearly desired to convict perceptive readers about God's nature and His ways.

In the book of Jonah, for example, we have noticed many subtle concepts, such as how God deals with all people—whether in or outside the covenant line—with the same standard of justice. The author never explicitly mentions or defines this issue, but instead reveals it indirectly through the repetition of key words and phrases and through the use of irony and subtle comparison. In fact, when readers pay careful attention to the many details of the book of Jonah, they will realize that ultimately the story is about the magnificent God of heaven and earth. The biblical author reveals so many of His attributes in just four brief chapters.

We need to review an important principle at this juncture. When Holy Scripture speaks of God, it does not attempt to prove His existence. No biblical writer ever expresses any doubt that God exists.

Nor do they derive their descriptions about Him from their imagination. Instead, without hesitancy they fill the pages of Scripture with detailed depictions of God acting within human history. The book of Jonah is part of this vast panorama.

We can be grateful that God, the true "author" of Scripture, superintended not only the content but also the formation of the canon and thereby made sure that it included the book of Jonah. For this particular Bible book makes a major contribution to the biblical picture of God. Consider how the book enhances our understanding of Him.

1. *God's knowledge.* His understanding of His creation and His creatures is intimate and inclusive. God remains vitally involved in nature and in the very lives of His creatures. In the book of Jonah the Old Testament reaches one of its highest points in revealing God in His relationship to creation and history and His tender concern for all His creatures. With God's final question to Jonah ("Should I not pity Nineveh—and what about the animals?" [see Jonah 4:11]) we find one of the most amazing biblical glimpses of the personhood of God and His involvement in our human situation. Our own human concern about others is nothing when compared to God's.

2. *God's sovereign power.* The book of Jonah dramatically reminds us that God's sovereignty is far greater than we might expect. Even the pagan mariners of chapter 1 recognized that the powerful "great storm" resulted from more than just natural causes. And that dangerous tempest drew their attention to the great God of heaven and earth.

The book of Jonah underscores the biblical understanding that no pagan god can compare in any way with the true God. The decisive and powerful actions of Yahweh throughout Scripture stand in stark contrast to all other deities. Unlike human idols, the God of the book of Jonah has the power to do something that really matters. All through the book of Jonah the author reminds the reader of God's power and His constant providence over His creation.

"The Lord is in active communication with every part of His vast dominion. He is represented as bending toward the earth and its inhabitants. He is listening to every word that is uttered. He hears every groan; He listens to every prayer; He observes the movements of every one."[1]

3. *God's forgiving nature.* He is always surprising human beings by His capacity and inclination to forgive. Jonah had a hard time grasping this. The divine propensity for forgiveness must be a difficult thing for sinful human beings to appreciate, for Jesus Himself spent much time talking about God's forgiveness. All four Gospels frequently recount that God is far more generous with His forgiveness than many of us think. Even Christ's parables often draw attention to this.

For example, the parable of the prodigal son could be called the parable of the forgiving father (Luke 15:11-32). The parable of the employer who gives the workers hired at the eleventh hour a full day's wage also draws attention to the extreme generosity of the nature of salvation (Matt. 20:1-16). Jesus described how human parents, sinful though they are, know how to shower their children with good things. He then draws the analogy that God, the heavenly Father, is even more generous and loving. If we ask God for bread, we will certainly not get a stone (Matt. 7:7-11).

The book of Jonah is one of the most profound pictures of God's forgiveness in Scripture. Perhaps that is the reason our Jewish brothers and sisters read the book at *minchah,* the afternoon service on the Day of Atonement, close to the holiest hour when Yom Kippur nears its peak. In the holy day's final hours, when judgment is about to close, they recite the book of Jonah, for it ends with God Himself declaring His inclination to forgive.

4. *God's moral nature.* We observe the divine system of morality all through the book of Jonah. God consistently deals on an equal basis with Jonah, the pagan sailors, and the Ninevites. The book of Jonah, as all Scripture, links religion and morality in the closest possible way. In fact, the Bible knows nothing of morality apart from religion. The entire canon stresses the importance of doing righteousness. Christ Himself affirmed this when He said, "If you love Me, you will keep My commandments" (John 14:15, NASB). Much earlier God declared to Abraham, "Know for certain that your descendants will be strangers in a land that is not theirs, where they will be enslaved and oppressed four hundred years. *But I will also judge the nation whom they will serve;* and afterward they will come out with many possessions. And as for you, you shall go to your fathers in

peace; you shall be buried at a good old age. Then in the fourth generation they shall return here, *for the iniquity of the Amorite is not yet complete"* (Gen. 15:13-16, NASB). Even the wicked pagan Ninevites, when they came under God's judgment, acknowledged the correctness of the divine sentence. The king of Nineveh himself reminded the citizenry of their violence and wickedness. Scripture commonly uses the expression "walking uprightly" to refer to the moral life, no matter what the nationality.

5. *God is a personal being.* The Lord participates in personal relationships in the book of Jonah. One whole chapter consists of a conversation between Him and Jonah. The biblical author never represents God as an abstract idea or some vague impersonal power. He is not a distant being barely involved with the people on this earth. Nor is He a cosmic dictator who seeks uncomprehending and silent submission on the part of His subjects. All through Scripture we find Him pleading and reasoning with human beings. God seeks intimate relationships in which men and women enter as freely as He does Himself. In addition to Jonah, we could review many biblical examples, including the book of Job. When God responds to Job's questionings, His reply fills up four chapters (Job 38, 39, 40, 41). In the New Testament Jesus treated the ostracized Samaritans and pagan Gentiles as valued people, something the Old Testament prophets had regularly insisted upon.

6. *God is judge.* The biblical teaching on judgment is vital, and the book of Jonah offers an important testimony to it. When God summons a people or nation to judgment, He is not merely vindictive. Rather, through His strong warnings, He seeks to awaken the conscience. In the book of Jonah He called a wicked and violent city into judgment so that they might turn from their evil ways and be saved. He delighted to forget their past acts of rebellion. Even the psalmist felt constrained to compose hymns about God's merciful nature: "As far as the east is from the west, so far has He removed our transgressions from us. As a father pities his children, so the Lord pities those who fear Him. For He knows our frame; He remembers that we are dust" (Ps. 103:12-14).

The God revealed in Scripture is not a deity who deprives human beings of their liberty, as with the human despots that humanity often has to endure. Only those with a totally wrong concept of God's character would even suggest otherwise.

Sometimes people describe the God of the Old Testament as wrathful and incalculable. But if one were to ask Abraham and Sarah, Job, Moses, and Isaiah how they would characterize God, surely they would respond that He is a deity who speaks and listens. Biblical figures, including Jonah, frequently question God. God Himself invites us to "come now, and let us reason together" (Isa. 1:18).

In the New Testament God continues His desire to dialogue. Jesus constantly interacts with all kinds of people. Some of the many recorded conversations of Jesus include those with Nicodemus (John 3); the Samaritan woman (John 4); the Syrophoenician mother (Mark 7:24-37); and Peter (John 21:15-17). Christ always graciously gave human beings time and room to listen thoughtfully and respond. He allowed them to dispute His Word, or even not listen at all. Our Savior never communicated in a way that forced anyone simply to hear and assent mindlessly.

When God chose not to punish Nineveh, His character did not really change. The judgment message had as its divine goal the conversion of the Ninevites so that He would not have to punish them. God's threatenings are often conditional. The Lord Himself said so through Jeremiah:

"At what instant I shall speak concerning a nation, and concerning a kingdom, to pluck up, and to pull down, and to destroy it; if that nation, against whom I have pronounced, turn from their evil, I will repent of the evil that I thought to do unto them" (Jer. 18:7, 8, KJV).

Some still talk about the inherent goodness in human beings. But Scripture continually reminds us that this is nonsense. Isaiah, Jeremiah, Paul, and James are but a few of the many Bible writers who, along with the book of Jonah, insist this important point:

"For all of us have become like one who is unclean, and all our righteous deeds are like a filthy garment" (Isa. 64:6, NASB).

"Can the Ethiopian change his skin or the leopard his spots? Then you also can do good who are accustomed to do evil" (Jer. 13:23, NASB).

"[Man's] throat is an open sepulchre" (Rom. 3:13, KJV).

All Scripture, and particularly the narratives, instruct us that human beings left to themselves will always fall to lower levels, with the next generations plunging yet further down. "Professing to be wise, they became fools" (Rom. 1:23, NASB). The Bible truthfully presents the reality of sinful human nature. Even the pagan Ninevites, when confronted with God's judgment, acknowledged their wickedness. And the king himself felt the need for repentance.

7. *God is love.* The book of Jonah reminds us of God's overwhelming love for all of His creation. He expresses this Himself in the last verse of the book of Jonah with His mention of the animals as one of His reasons to show mercy to Nineveh. God also included the animal kingdom as He responded to Job's questions. Philip Yancey is right:

"God loves matter. You can read his signature everywhere: rocks that crack open to reveal delicate crystals, the clouds swirling around Venus, the fecundity of the oceans (home to 90 percent of all living things). Clearly, according to Genesis, the act of creation gave God pleasure."[2]

This should alert us to how the heart of God must ache when He sees humanity recklessly destroying the glories of His creation: the rain forests, our water supply, the elephants and the whales; or His children destroying their minds with drugs and promiscuous behavior. All this is bad enough. But even more horrifying is the fact that it caused the pain of losing His Son.

We generally calculate the fall of Adam and Eve in terms of its effects on us. Perhaps we need to think more of how it hurt God. The Bible devotes the first two chapters to the glories of the original creation. All the rest that follows reveals the agonizing course God has had to take to restore His creation to His original plan.

Yes, God is love. But the book of Jonah instructs us that His steadfast love is not that of benign neglect, nor does He exist simply to guarantee our happiness. James Edwards is right when he declares:

"One of the surprising truths of the Bible is that God is not necessarily 'nice.' This has often been misunderstood. We like to imagine a God who champions our 'rights,' who exists for the purposes of our self-fulfillment and prosperity—a God who holds people accountable to a standard that differs from their own will, or who demands obedience to a revealed will that confronts and conflicts with their selfish pleasures, is less attractive. . . .

"If the happiness of others is our sole concern, then it is probably safe to say that we care very little for them. We never practice such superficial benevolence toward those for whom we really care. . . . Love wills for the other more than simply happiness. It is no different with God."[3]

8. *The truth about God.* An issue that the church faces each generation is how to present God in a contemporary manner. One of the tempting ways is to bring Him down to where people will say, "Oh, I like that kind of God." We are sometimes afraid to make people face the true God of Scripture. One of the tragedies of our present time is that some Christians are capitulating to an attitude of pluralism, saying, "It really doesn't matter. There are Buddhists, Hindus, and Christians, but we are all trying to get to the same place."

The book of Jonah speaks directly to this issue, for that is where the sailors in chapter 1 were. Each of them was crying to "his god." But then something happened. And it led them to call upon the true God—a God who was all-powerful, a God who was there.

Thus we can learn from the book of Jonah that we never need apologize for the God of Scripture. People may scoff. But if they are ever truly converted, they will have been confronted by the true God, as we see graphically in the story of Jonah. Both the non-Israelite sailors and later the violent Ninevites all found themselves convicted to call upon the name of the true God. And we learn how the Word of God can lead even violent pagans to forsake their evil ways when given a chance.

9. *God's deep yearnings.* The book of Jonah teaches us that God longs to be known by us far more than we want to know Him. His great work in us is to increase our passion for knowing Him until it is stronger than anything else in life. Developing that passion in our hearts is a long, difficult process for both God and us. But He is relentlessly committed to it. Jonah's experience teaches us that if nothing else. The way may be hard, but the journey is worth it.

Unfortunately, just as with Jonah, we modern Christians are often more interested in finding ourselves than in finding God. Understanding ourselves has become the highest virtue in modern culture. As Christian psychologist Larry Crabb writes:

"We have become committed to relieving the pain behind our problems rather than using our pain to wrestle more passionately with the character and purposes of God. *Feeling better has become more important than finding God.* And worse, we assume that people who find God always feel better."[4]

As human beings we relate to God the way we might to a waiter in a restaurant. We like attentive treatment, but exceptional treatment deserves special recognition. And certainly God qualifies for that. He has gone to great trouble to help us. Therefore we leave Him a "big tip" and, feeling benevolent and grateful, tell Him, "Well done! Your service has been excellent."

But this is backwards! We think that God is worthy of honor because He has saved and honored us. Instead, we need to remind ourselves often that the primary issue at stake in Christianity is not us, but rather the God who created and redeemed us, a fact taught all through Scripture. One of the Genesis genealogies even illustrates this: "After he begot Methuselah, Enoch walked with God three hundred years" (Gen. 5:22).

The others listed in the genealogy Scripture describes as merely "living." But Enoch "walked with God." This subtle contrast in the genealogy is significant. The prospect of walking with God should stagger us. It should take our breath away. We, like Enoch, can really walk with God!

The prophet Amos brings up the same issue: "Can two walk together, except they be agreed?" (Amos 3:3, KJV).

If we are to walk with God, one thing becomes immediately clear in Scripture: we must go in the same direction He does. As we saw with Jonah, God doesn't negotiate. Instead He invites us to join Him. And His course is clear. He has committed Himself to "[gathering] together in one all things in Christ, both of which are in heaven, and which are on earth; even in him" (Eph. 1:10, KJV). To walk with God, we have no option but to join Him on that path. It requires that we make every other ambition in our hearts secondary and abandon anything that contradicts God's purpose. Jonah learned this the hard way.

We need to ask ourselves whether we are merely seeking to arrange our lives around getting our needs met, or if we are truly committed to knowing God and thus cooperating with Him in a divine plan much larger than ourselves.

This is what makes so many of the people in the biblical narratives so appealing. Reading the stories of their lives, we get the strong impression that these men and women knew God in a way we don't yet. Scripture reveals ordinary people—weak, stumbling, sinful people—who sought a relationship with the Lord and stayed with it. People such as Hannah, who is in a difficult marital arrangement at a time when even the "church" leaders are particularly sinful; Daniel, a teenage prisoner of war who determines to remain true to God at the risk of his life; Hosea , who proclaims God's compassion even though an unfaithful wife has shattered his own heart; Habakkuk, who exults in the Lord (Hab. 3:18) while trembling with terror over his country's imminent destruction. The hatred of friends and fellow citizens couldn't quench God's fire in Jeremiah's heart. And Peter was so moved with the meaning of Christ's sacrifice that he didn't feel worthy to die in the same upright position as his Lord, thus requesting his executioner to crucify him upside down. All of these experiences, along with Jonah's, can instruct our own!

10. *The nature of salvation*. The literary structure of this book places Jonah's statement "Salvation is of the Lord" (Jonah 2:9) at the climax of his prayer and the center of the book. This alerts us to the central meaning that the writer intended by structuring the book in a chiasm, or "mirror writing," as we saw earlier. The book of Jonah is not about the "great fish," but rather about the "great God"! He brings salvation to the pagan sailors in chapter 1. The Lord brings Jonah to the place where he then expresses this profound truth in chapter 2. God next saves the whole city of wicked Ninevites in chapter 3. And in chapter 4 God Himself expresses and emphasizes His merciful nature.

Not only that, the book of Jonah also shows how God converts sinners to Himself. The book is one of the most evangelistic in the entire Bible. It reveals how God saves people. Even petulant Jonah felt constrained to admit it even though it offended him: "I know that You are a gracious and merciful God, slow to anger and abundant in lovingkindness, One who relents from doing harm" (Jonah 4:2).

The book then concludes with a final question. But it never tells us how Jonah responded. Perhaps this open-ended question draws us to ponder more about the meaning of book, and even to apply its profound lessons to ourselves.

The book of Jonah may be one of the "minor prophets," but it is definitely not in the "minor leagues." It demands concentrated attention to probe its depths. As we have seen, the book is not about the "great fish" or, ultimately, even about Jonah himself. Rather, it opens and concludes with the Word of God to one of His erring children. And in between it gives us one of the clearest pictures of God's universal love, sovereignty, and redemption anywhere in Scripture.

"Let the heavens rejoice, and let
    the earth be glad;
And let them say among the nations,
    'The Lord reigns.'
Let the sea roar, and all its fullness;
Let the field rejoice, and all that is in it.
Then the trees of the woods shall
    rejoice before the Lord,
For He is coming to judge the earth.
Oh, give thanks to the Lord, for He is good!
For His mercy endures forever"
                    (1 Chron. 16:31-34).

---

[1] E. G. White, *Our Father Cares* (Hagerstown, Md.: Review and Herald Pub. Assn., 1991), pp. 56, 57.

[2] Philip Yancey, *Finding God in Unexpected Places* (Ann Arbor, Mich.: Servant Publications, 1997), p. 37.

[3] J. R. Edwards, *The Divine Intruder*, p. 95.

[4] Larry Crabb, Jr., *Finding God* (Grand Rapids: Zondervan Pub. House, 1993), p. 18. His rich insights inform this whole section.